Mary Todd Lincoln

FIRST LADY OF CONTROVERSY

Text by

Thomas F. Schwartz

Foreword by

Rick Beard

Published by

Springfield, Illinois

2007

PUBLISHER'S NOTE

Mary Todd Lincoln: First Lady of Controversy is published in conjunction with an exhibition of the same name held at the Abraham Lincoln Presidential Museum from April 28 through November 28, 2007.

A special thank you goes to James M. Cornelius for his assistance in editing the text and to the Batavia Historical Society and the Mary Todd Lincoln House for permission to publish images from their collections

© 2007 Abraham Lincoln Presidential Library Foundation

Abraham Lincoln Presidential Library Foundation
500 East Madison, Suite 200
Springfield, IL 62701
www.alplm.org

FOREWORD

Mary Todd Lincoln was the first American president's wife to be dubbed "First Lady" and to this day she remains one of the most controversial spouses ever to occupy the White House. During her life, she was loved and hated, praised and vilified. The nature of her marriage, her influence on Abraham Lincoln, her success as a mother and a wife, her role in the White House, her sometimes questionable judgment, and her physical and mental health have all been topics of debate for 150 years.

Mary Todd's life began amid a mixture of material comfort and emotional want, and Mrs. Lincoln's ended on a note of intense bereavement. Born into a well-to-do, politically connected Kentucky family, she lost her mother as a young girl and found her new stepmother to be remote and unloving. Well educated, attractive, and vivacious, Mary did not want for suitors. She found in Abraham Lincoln her match in intelligence and devotion to politics, and historical claims that she saw in him a future president seem credible. With his ascension to the office in 1861, Mary found herself moving in the most powerful circles in America. Within four years, she had paid an unbearable price—a beloved son lost to typhoid and a husband martyred by an assassin's bullet. By the time of her death, Mary had become a figure to be pitied—alienated from her only surviving son, who had her declared insane and for a brief time institutionalized, and riven with anxiety about her personal financial situation.

Historical certainty eludes us as we consider Mary Todd Lincoln. Many historians, taking their lead from William Herndon, have portrayed Mary as a harridan, a spoiled spendthrift, anything but a helpmate to her husband. Others credit her with Lincoln's rise and suggest that, as a strong woman in the male-dominated world of the nineteenth century, she has been unfairly demonized. What is undeniable is that she remains a "first lady of controversy." This catalogue and the exhibition it complements encourage you to explore the evidence and reach your own conclusion.

Thanks are due to Dr. Thomas Schwartz, Illinois State Historian and Lincoln expert nonpareil, who authored the text and captions and selected the illustrations for this book. Thanks also to Susan Mogerman, Chief Operating Officer of the Abraham Lincoln Presidential Library Foundation, who oversaw all aspects of the design and production of the publication, and to the Foundation, which generously underwrote all costs associated with the project.

The reader will note that many of the objects and documents illustrated in the following pages are from the Collection of Louise and Barry Taper. Mary Todd was Lincoln's first lady, and it is surely no exaggeration to characterize Ms. Taper as the "first lady of Lincoln." Her devotion to gathering and preserving the material evidence of our greatest president and his family has resulted in the creation of a truly national treasure. We are grateful for her generosity in allowing us to share a small portion of her collection with the public.

Rick Beard

Executive Director
Abraham Lincoln Presidential Library and Museum
June 2007

Oil painting, portrait from life of Mary Lincoln by Jerome Fielding, 1865.
(Abraham Lincoln Presidential Library and Museum)

MY OLD KENTUCKY HOME

MY OLD KENTUCKY HOME

Mary Ann Todd was born on December 13, 1818, to Eliza Parker Todd and Robert Smith Todd in Lexington, Kentucky. She was the fourth child born into a distinguished lineage, joining siblings Elizabeth, Frances, and Levi.

The Todds traced their ancestors to a Scottish clan. The Scottish word for "fox" is a variation of "Todd," hence the use of a fox on the family coat of arms given to Thomas Todd in 1490 by King Henry VII. The Todd clan fled Scotland for northern Ireland to escape religious persecution. Robert Todd, Mary's great-great grandfather, was born in Ireland but resettled in Pennsylvania. General Levi Todd, Mary's grandfather, was born in Pennsylvania, studied law and surveying in Virginia, and eventually relocated to Kentucky. There he gained fame as a military man and became one of the important founders of the city of Lexington, serving as the first clerk of the Fayette county court. He continued to play a prominent role in the history of the city, state, and region until his death in 1807.

General Levi Todd's seventh child was Robert Smith Todd, who was born outside Lexington, Kentucky, on February 25, 1791. Given his family's status, Robert was brought up in an environment of books and learning. He entered Transylvania University in Lexington at age fourteen. Upon graduation Robert worked on the staff of Thomas Bodley, clerk of the Fayette circuit court, and studied law with George M. Bibb, chief justice of the Kentucky court of appeals. He fought in the War of 1812 with the Fifth Regiment Kentucky Volunteers. Upon his return from the war, he joined with fellow veteran Bird Smith in establishing the grocery of Smith & Todd. Later he invested in Oldham, Todd & Company, a cotton-yarn and fabric manufacturer with customers throughout the Ohio River valley. Robert S. Todd's business flourished, providing him the means to enter politics by the time he was thirty years old. He served twenty years as clerk of the Kentucky House of Representatives and was elected to the Kentucky state senate in 1845.

Robert Smith Todd married well. His first wife, Eliza Ann Parker, the grand-daughter of General Andrew Porter, came from one of Lexington's most wealthy and prominent families. Eliza was also a cousin to Robert Todd. By all accounts, the marriage was marked by happiness.

Mary's childhood was one of material wealth but emotional want. Her father's career ambitions kept him away from home for long periods of time. Eliza devoted what time she could to her children, but frequently her mother's slaves were called upon to help with household chores and to attend to the children. Mammy Sally, a black servant, served as a more fearsome authority figure than either of Mary's parents.

Shortly after the birth of the couple's sixth child, George Rogers Clark Todd, Eliza died on July 6, 1825. Mary Ann Todd was not yet seven years old. Robert asked his unmarried sister, Ann Maria, to come and help him raise his children. Within months of Eliza's death, Robert was courting Elizabeth "Betsey" Humphreys, who also came from a very prominent Lexington family. They were married on November 1, 1826, and Betsey would give birth to nine children.

The death of Eliza was a deep loss for her children. Their father's seemingly immediate marriage to Betsey added to the bewilderment. The situation was further confused when Eliza's mother, Elizabeth Porter Parker, expressed her dissatisfaction with her son-in-law's new wife. Eliza's children gravitated toward the grandmother as their protector, while Betsey focused on her responsibilities to her own growing family. The line of demarcation between the two sets of children continued well beyond Robert Todd's death.

Robert Smith Todd supported a rigorous education for his daughters in the belief that it would make them more appealing to young suitors and also provide them with the skills to teach the next generation of leaders. Mary was sent to the academy of Dr. John Ward, where she spent four years largely reciting lessons. At fourteen, she entered the boarding school of Madame Mentelle, a French refugee who taught Mary fluent French, instilled in her a love for the arts, and provided her with a solid education.

Ward's academy was located across from Henry Clay's mansion, Ashland. Clay's Whig politics comported well with Robert Todd's own views, and the two men were close friends socially and politically. Mary grew up seeing all of the leading political figures of Kentucky at public events and as guests in her father's house. Her interest in politics and political debate took root as a young woman and never diminished with time.

Sibling rivalries exist in all families, and Mary and her sisters were no exception.

Mary appeared to get along well with her two older sisters, Elizabeth and Frances. From Ann, Mary remained more distant. Siblings can resent the shift in attention to a newborn, and in this instance, Mary also lost the use of her name. Born Mary Ann Todd, she dropped the "Ann" when sister Ann Maria Todd was born.

Oil painting of Mary Todd by Katherine Helm, Mary Todd's niece.
(The Collection of Louise and Barry Taper)

Oil painting of Robert Smith Todd, Mary Todd's father,
by Katherine Helm
after an original portrait painting by Matthew Jouett.
(Abraham Lincoln Presidential Library and Museum)

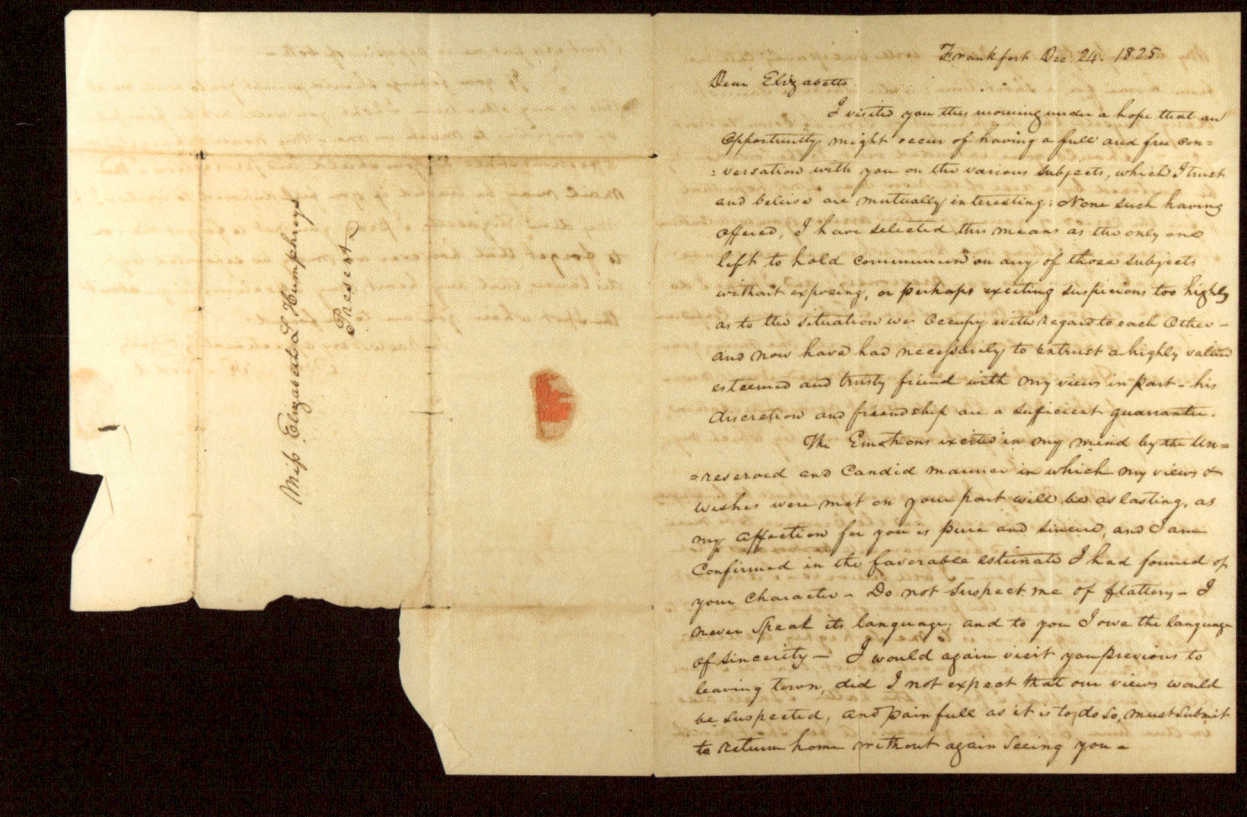

Robert Smith Todd, autograph letter signed,
to Elizabeth Humphreys, December 24, 1825.
(The Collection of Louise and Barry Taper)

Less than six months after Mary's mother died, her father is already seeking to remarry. The marriage would take place in 1826, distancing Mary and her sisters from their stepmother.

SPRINGFIELD

SPRINGFIELD

In an 1866 interview with William Henry Herndon, Abraham Lincoln's law partner, Mary Todd Lincoln recalled that her first visit to Springfield, Illinois, was in 1837. Recent archival discoveries show that her first visit occurred two years earlier. The circumstances surrounding the visit are murky, but it is plausible that she and her older sister Frances accompanied their father on a business trip to Springfield. Robert Smith Todd speculated in Illinois land and had extensive business interests in the state. It also provided him an opportunity to visit his eldest daughter, Elizabeth, and her husband Ninian Wirt Edwards.

Clearly the Edwards home in Springfield offered the daughters of Eliza Parker Todd a safe haven from the oversight of Betsey Humphreys Todd. Elizabeth Edwards later recalled that they left Lexington because "of the circumstances that rendered life unpleasant in our father's home. Mary left home to avoid living under the same roof with her stepmother." While visits to Springfield helped relieve tensions in Lexington, Mary had to wait until her sister Frances wed Dr. William Wallace on May 21, 1839, before she had a room of her own at the Edwards home.

Springfield offered none of the glamour of Lexington, Kentucky. It was nestled in the vast Illinois prairie along an old Indian route that connected Alton to Peoria. White settlers later renamed the route Edwards Trace after Ninian Edwards, the first territorial governor and father of Ninian Wirt Edwards. The rapid growth of Illinois in the 1830s brought a great influx of settlers from the East as well as many from Kentucky, Tennessee, and Virginia. Mary found sons, grandsons, cousins, and shirt-tail relations of all kinds migrating to Illinois and to Springfield in particular. Besides her sisters Elizabeth and Frances, Mary's uncle Dr. John Todd resided in Springfield, along with her cousin John Todd Stuart, one of the leading lawyers and a prominent Whig politician. The migration of new settlers in Illinois also necessitated the relocation of the state capital to the more populous region of central Illinois. Of all the communities that vied for the honor, Springfield was selected to be the new capital city, beating out more notable rivals Alton and Jacksonville, and perhaps the more appropriate contender, the town of Purgatory.

Construction of a new capitol building brought new life and vitality to the community. Merchants sensing opportunity moved to the city, and improvements of every kind were discussed. In spite of local booster visions for Springfield, its citizens were reminded daily of the grim realities of city life. It was not uncommon for residents to be confronted with hogs wandering freely in the streets, rooting up the plank sidewalks, wallowing in the rain-soaked dirt roads, and leaving behind fragrant reminders of their presence. The spring rains turned the dirt roads and pedestrian paths into thick, sticky mud bogs.

Mere mud could not stop Mary, though. Having grown weary of remaining cooped up indoors, Mary and her friend Mercy Levering decided to tackle the mud and ventured outside. Determined to walk to the square, Mary and Mercy grabbed wooden shingles and created their own plank walkway. The plan worked fine until the shingles ran out. They could not retrace their steps since many of the shingles had disappeared in the mud. Luckily a wagon came by to offer assistance. Dr. E. H. Merriman "Riding on a Dray" immortalized the incident in poem:

> As I walked out on Monday Last
> A wet and muddy day
> 'Twas there I saw a pretty lass
> A riding on a dray, a riding on a dray.
> Quoth I sweet lass, what do you there
> Said she good lack a day
> I had no coach to take me home
> So I'm riding on a dray
> Next door to Mr. Hay
> By yellow Poll's and Spottswood then
> A riding on a dray.
> The ragged boys threw up their caps
> And poor folks ran away
> As by James Lamb's and o'er the bridge
> I plodded on my way
> Up flew windows, out popped heads,
> To see this Lady gay
> In silken cloak and feathers white
> A riding on a dray
> At length arrived at Edwards' gate
> Hart backed the usual way
> And taking out the iron pin
> He rolled her off the dray.
> When safely landed on her feet
> Said she what is to pay
> Quoth Hart I cannot charge you aught
> For riding on my dray
> An honor such as this
> I meet not every day
> For surely I'm the happiest man
> That every drove a dray.
> A moral I'll append
> To this my humble lay
> When you are sticking in the mud
> Why call out for a dray.

If Mary's unique sense of adventure often ran contrary to social convention, her advanced education, interest in political issues, refined manners, lively spirit, uncommonly attractive looks, and superb conversational skills made her the envy of many around her. Ninian Wirt Edwards boasted that "Mary could make a bishop forget his prayers." Indeed, she attracted numerous suitors, including Stephen A. Douglas, Edwin Webb, and Abraham Lincoln. Scholars divide over whether Douglas was serious about a relationship with Mary. Edwin Webb relentlessly pursued Mary, but she did not find appealing the prospect of marrying a widower fifteen years her senior with two children.

Eventually she found herself increasingly drawn to the least likely suitor, Abraham Lincoln. The six-foot-four-inch Springfield lawyer and legislator towered over Mary's five-foot-four-inch frame. Universally recognized as an intelligent and shrewd lawyer and politician, Lincoln was known for his great warmth and love for storytelling. His awkwardness around women was legendary, as Mary soon learned firsthand. Yet there was a physical and emotional connection that brought the two together. And their mutual interest in the Whig politics of Henry Clay gave them plenty of grist for discussion. They also shared an interest in poetry, especially that of Robert Burns and the sonnets of William Shakespeare.

At some point the couple became engaged or had an understanding that marriage was on the horizon. The marriage was opposed by Ninian and Elizabeth Edwards, who "warned Mary that she and Mr. Lincoln were not suitable." "Mr. Edwards and myself," said Elizabeth, "believed they were different in nature, and education and raising . . . They were so different that they could not live happily as man and wife." Typically, scholars point to Abraham Lincoln's reference of "that fatal first of Jan'y. '41" as marking the estrangement and breakup of the relationship with Mary. Lincoln clearly went through an extended period of depression, claiming "I am now the most miserable man living. If what I feel were equally distributed to the whole human family, there would not be one cheerful face on earth. Whether I shall ever be better I can not tell; I awfully forbode I shall not. To remain as I am is impossible; I must die or be better it appears to me." Mary complained to Mercy Levering during the summer of 1841 that Lincoln "deems me unworthy of notice, as I have not met him in the gay world for months . . ."

The intervention of friends the following year probably encouraged reconciliation. Eliza and Simeon Francis are credited with providing their residence as a secret meeting place for the young couple, away from the disapproving eyes of Ninian and Elizabeth Edwards.

A series of anonymous letters criticizing General James Shields, the Illinois state auditor, began to appear in the *Sangamo Journal* in August 1842. Shields refused to accept state bank scrip for payment of taxes, leading Whigs to poke fun at him and other Democratic officeholders. Mary and a friend, Julie Jayne, joined in submitting their own anonymous gibes at Shields. The public ridicule so angered Shields that he demanded to know who was behind the anonymous attacks. Lincoln stepped forward and accepted the blame. Shields challenged Lincoln to a duel, and Lincoln, steering clear of pistols that might injure both men, selected broadswords in hopes of deterring a conflict. Illegal in Illinois, duels were usually fought on Bloody Island, on the Missouri side of the Mississippi River across from Alton, Illinois. Fortunately, cooler minds prevailed, just as both Shields and Lincoln had hoped.

With the aborted duel behind them, Abraham Lincoln and Mary Todd were married in the parlor of the Edwards home on November 4, 1842. Mary wore the wedding skirt of her sister Frances, and Abraham gave her a gold wedding band from Chatterton jewelry store that carried the inscription "Love is Eternal."

Wedding skirt worn by Mary Todd on her marriage to Abraham Lincoln, November 4, 1842.
(Abraham Lincoln Presidential Library and Museum)

The skirt was a hand-me-down given to Mary from her sister, Frances Todd Wallace.

Tablecloth given as a wedding present
to Abraham and Mary Lincoln
from Ninian and Elizabeth Todd Edwards.
(Abraham Lincoln Presidential Library and Museum)

Battle Axe and Political Reformer, November 19, 1842.
(The Collection of Louise and Barry Taper)

This newspaper describes both Lincoln's duel with
Shields and his marriage to Mary Todd.

Abraham Lincoln, autograph letter signed,
to Joshua Fry Speed, October 5, 1842.
(Abraham Lincoln Presidential Library and Museum)

Lincoln writes, "You have heard of my duel with
Shields, and I have now to inform you that the duelling
business still rages in this city."

Coin silver spoons, Platt & Brother, New York circa 1825.
(The Collection of Louise and Barry Taper)

These American fiddle pattern spoons were owned by Elizabeth
Edwards and may have been used in the wedding service for
Abraham and Mary Lincoln at the Edwards home.

FIRST LADY OF CONTROVERSY

The Lincoln Family in 1861, photograph
of oil painting by Francis Bicknell Carpenter.
(Abraham Lincoln Presidential Library and Museum)

WIFE AND MOTHER

WIFE AND MOTHER

The newlyweds began their marriage by renting a room at the Globe Tavern at Adams and Third streets in Springfield. Dr. William and Frances Wallace had spent their first months of marriage at this same hotel, setting the precedent for the Todd sisters.

Lincoln went right to his law work following the wedding, but paused to sum up his feelings in a letter to a legal colleague a week after his marriage: "Nothing new here, except my marrying, which to me, is matter of profound wonder." Mary continued to meet with her girlfriends and joined many of Springfield's curious in attending the habeas corpus proceeding of Joseph Smith in the federal court room near the square. Like most young couples, Abraham and Mary Lincoln used this time to save money for a house and plan for the future. By March 24, 1843, Lincoln had alerted his friend Joshua Speed that Mary was pregnant. On August 1, 1843, Robert Todd Lincoln was born. His healthy lungs were undoubtedly the reason that the Lincolns sought new living quarters. They found a rental cottage at 214 South Fourth Street, where they lived during the winter of 1843-44. In January 1844, Lincoln was negotiating a contract with the Reverend Charles Dresser, the Episcopal minister who presided at the Lincoln marriage ceremony, to purchase his one-and-a-half-story cottage on the corner of Eighth and Jackson streets. By early May the deal was completed and the contract inked at a sale price of $1,500.

The home provided Abraham and Mary a place where they could raise their family and retreat from the demands of public life. The structure was enlarged to keep up with the growing family. At least four expansions to the residence pushed the home out, back, and up, so that by the mid-1850s it was a full two stories and could accommodate their family of three sons. Much of the money for the renovations came from Lincoln's legal practice. His annual income, believed to have ranged from $3,000 to $5,000, was well above the income of a farmer or laborer. The home's major expansion in the 1850s was financed by the sale of 80 acres of land presented to Mary by her father.

Robert Smith Todd visited the couple after the birth of Robert Todd Lincoln, his namesake, and provided Mary and Abraham with financial assistance to hire a servant. Smith also was desirous to promote Lincoln's political ambitions, writing in March 1844 to Ninian Wirt Edwards: "I can use influence here if Mr. Clay is elected (of which there can be no doubt) to procure some appointment for him which will keep him out of Congress until his Situation in a monied point of view, will enable him to take a stand in Congress, creditable both to himself and Country. Such as District Attorney or Judge."

On March 10, 1846, Mary gave birth to another son, Edward Baker Lincoln, named after a prominent Springfield Whig politician and Lincoln associate, Edward Dickinson Baker. Eddie remained a sickly child and would succumb to pulmonary tuberculosis on February 1, 1850. In spite of Mary's constant ministrations, there was nothing that nineteenth-century medicine could do to cure Eddie's ailment. His death was emotionally devastating for both parents. Mary overcame her grief by taking instruction and formally joining the First Presbyterian Church, where the Lincolns would eventually rent a pew and later baptize their son Thomas. Her husband did not join the church but found comfort in discussions with the Reverend James Smith, who, like Lincoln, had been a religious skeptic early in his life.

Part of the healing process from Eddie's death was to fill the void with another child. William Wallace Lincoln came into the world on December 21, 1850, and was named for Mary's brother-in-law, Dr. William Wallace. Willie became the unspoken favorite of both parents because of his intelligence and winning personality. On April 4, 1853, a fourth son was born, whom they named Thomas after Abraham's late father. Nicknamed "Tad" as an infant because his large head and slim body resembled those of a tadpole, Tad probably suffered from a cleft palate that impaired his speech.

Children do not come with instruction manuals, and both Abraham and Mary learned the hard task of parenting by doing. Robert, being the first, received the most discipline, but Abraham and Mary quickly realized that even using the rod did not always produce the desired result. Writing to a friend, Lincoln described Robert as having "a great deal of that sort of mischief that is the offspring of much animal spirit. . . . Since I began this letter a messenger came to tell me Bob was lost; but by the time I reached the house, his mother had found him, and had him whiped, and by now, very likely he is run away again." With the rest of their sons the Lincolns were quite indulgent, allowing them great latitude, so much so that William Herndon wanted to "wring their necks." Most of the child-rearing responsibilities fell by default to Mary. Between Lincoln's legal practice, which took him away from home six months out of the year, and his political interests that could keep him on a campaign trail for longer periods, Mary was both mother and the head of the household.

Home life for Mary was both a blessing and a challenge. In her role as mother, Mary was responsible for providing the boys with a nurturing environment. She read the novels of Sir Walter Scott and the poems of Robert Burns to the boys and encouraged them to recite and perform for guests. She threw birthday parties for the boys and indulged them with candy. Although Mary was a fine seamstress, ready-made clothing was available from Springfield merchants and affordable for the middle class. Keeping the boys' clothing mended and in good repair was another matter. Fresh produce, eggs, butter, and milk were available at Springfield stores, saving Mary the trouble of raising her own garden vegetables, but the Lincolns did own a cow for fresh milk. There were fewer schooling options for the Lincoln boys than Mary had known in Lexington. Robert's attendance at the Illinois state university in Springfield did not prepare him adequately for Harvard, and he was forced to attend Phillips Exeter academy for a year before successfully passing Harvard's entrance exam.

Mary required help to run the Lincoln household. Good help was hard to come by, and she frequently had angry exchanges with the hired help, especially the "wild Irish." Most middle-class women found it difficult to obtain domestic help to assist with cleaning homes, washing laundry, preparing meals, canning fruits and vegetables for the winter, airing bedding, beating rugs, and all the other responsibilities that were demanded in keeping a home. Lacking reliable help and certain domestic skills, Mary purchased *Miss Leslie's House Book* and *Miss Leslie's Cookery* to fill the void. Mary kept an eye on costs and maintained strict economy, so much so that many hired girls thought her stingy. Unlike many middle-class Springfield residents who began to use gas lighting in the 1850s, Mary resisted, fearing a fire. She also feared lightning storms and insisted that lightning rods be added to the house.

While Mary resented Abraham's absences from home, she continued to support his political ambitions, hoping that he might become a United States senator. Lincoln's election to Congress in 1846 was seen as the beginning of a promising national career. It was decided that the entire family should go to Washington, D.C. Mary, Abraham, Robert, and Eddie left for Washington in October 1847, stopping first to visit the Todds in Lexington. Upon their arrival in Washington, it quickly became clear that the arrangement of having two small children in cramped boardinghouse quarters would not work. Mary took the boys with her back to Lexington. The letters that survive indicate the deep emotional bond shared by Abraham and Mary. Mary and the boys reunited with Abraham in the summer of 1848, traveling across New York State and visiting Niagara Falls. Although Lincoln's single congressional term was unremarkable, it whetted his appetite for higher office. In 1855 and again in 1858, Lincoln would attempt to secure a United States Senate seat. His lack of success for the Senate paid dividends by raising his profile among Republicans in Illinois and across the country. Mary assisted Lincoln in personalizing a form letter supporting John C. Frémont in the 1856 presidential campaign.

The debate over whether the Lincolns were happily married is endless. Evidence supports images of happiness and domestic bliss as well as Mary's volatile temper and Lincoln's self-absorption and aloofness. Statistically, the divorce rate in the decade of 1850–60 averaged 1.3% in Springfield. For public officials the rate stood at nearly 9%, reflecting the strain public life placed upon marriage. Whereas married life was a vast improvement for Abraham's quality of life, Mary witnessed a decline from the leisure and wealth of the Todd and Edwards households. Despite those pressures, the marriage survived to await Mary's next challenge: becoming first lady.

Daily Texts with Verses of Hymns,
American Tract Society, New York, n.d.
(The Collection of Louise and Barry Taper)

Inscribed by Mary Lincoln in 1852 to Mrs. Black
upon Black's joining the First Presbyterian Church

Mary Lincoln, autograph letter signed,
to Emily Helm, February 16, 1857.
(The Collection of Louise and Barry Taper)

Describes a party she gave sending out 500 invitations
"yet owing to an *unlucky* rain, 300 only favored us by their presence."

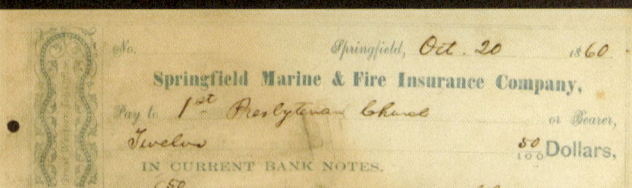

Abraham Lincoln, printed document signed,
pew rental check made out to the
First Presbyterian Church, October 20, 1860.
(The Collection of Louise and Barry Taper)

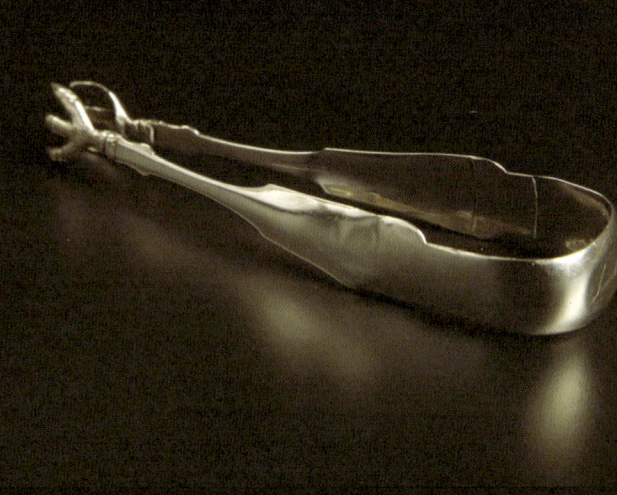

Sterling silver ice tongs owned by Abraham and Mary
Lincoln from G. W. Chatterton, Springfield, Illinois.
(The Collection of Louise and Barry Taper)

Mary Lincoln needle safe containing an image
of Abraham Lincoln among the patterned squares of cloth.
(The Collection of Louise and Barry Taper)

Mary Lincoln wicker sewing basket.
(Abraham Lincoln Presidential Library and Museum)

To economize, Mary mended the clothes of her sons
and embroidered her handkerchiefs.

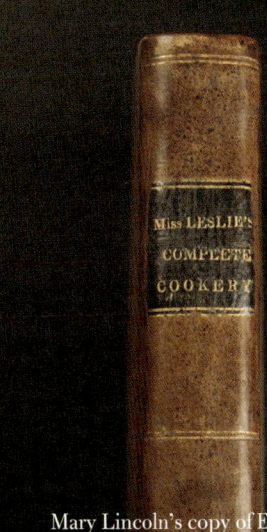

Mary Lincoln monogrammed tea napkin.
(The Collection of Louise and Barry Taper)

Mary Lincoln's copy of Eliza Leslie,
Directions for Cookery in its various branches…Philadelphia, 1840.
(The Collection of Louise and Barry Taper)

Accustomed to having servants cook her meals,
Mary had to take a crash course in meal planning
with this popular cookbook.

FIRST LADY OF CONTROVERSY 25

Mary Lincoln, photograph probably by Preston Butler, November 1860.
(Abraham Lincoln Presidential Library and Museum)

MRS. PRESIDENT LINCOLN

MRS. PRESIDENT LINCOLN

Abraham Lincoln did not campaign for the presidency in 1860, following the time-honored tradition that candidates should not actively seek the office but rather let the people call them to it. He stayed in Springfield using the home at Eighth and Jackson streets as a staging area for meetings and parades, such as the grand rally of August 8, 1860, with floats and hundreds of supporters. Lincoln also used rooms in the statehouse courtesy of Governor Wood. As streams of well-wishers came to Springfield to see the "Rail Splitter" from Illinois, shake his hand, or ask for his autograph, Mary found herself constantly entertaining and keeping the house presentable for special guests. She turned down an opportunity to accompany Adeline Judd, the wife of Norman B. Judd, head of the Illinois Republican Party, to Minnesota, pleading: "I am quite *unnerved* just now, and we have so much company, that I could scarcely leave home. . . ." Mary helped draft form letters that Lincoln signed for autograph seekers, and she occasionally sent letters to individuals to assuage their fears about her husband. The Reverend Dyer Burgess wished to vote for Lincoln, but only if he could be assured that Lincoln was not a member of a Masonic order or any other secret society. Mary obliged him by writing, "Mr. Lincoln has never been a Mason or belonged to any secret order . . ."

Mary both eagerly awaited and dreaded November 6, 1860, when the American voters would either embrace or reject her husband as president. When the returns from New York signaled a Republican victory, thousands of Springfield supporters cheered their favorite son. Celebrations were quickly replaced with the tasks associated with closing up the house in Springfield for the move to Washington, D.C. The Lincolns decided to purge the home of items that they no longer wanted by having a yard sale. Furniture that they favored was placed in storage, and the house was rented to the Tilton family. The Lincolns also burned old correspondence and records that were too bulky to keep. Not wanting to be seen as a hick from the West, Mary traveled to New York City in January of 1861 to buy attire appropriate for her new role as first lady. Amazed at the selection, high quality, and price of clothing, Mary often rationalized her extravagant spending as necessary to maintaining the dignity of the office. Merchants were only too willing to extend credit to her, and they often sent expensive items home with her that she chose to believe were gifts until the bills arrived later.

It was decided that Lincoln would leave Springfield on February 11, and Mary would take a later train with Willie and Tad and reunite with her husband in Indianapolis the following day. Death threats were constantly made against the president-elect, but he dismissed them as nothing more than harmless boasts. Mary took the threats more seriously, although she was determined not to be intimidated by them. When the train reached Pennsylvania, detective Allan Pinkerton met with Lincoln and his associates to inform them of a plot to attack Lincoln in Baltimore. Against his better judgment, Lincoln agreed to take an earlier train to Baltimore, where he needed to switch trains for Washington, D.C. Critics claimed that Lincoln sneaked into Washington because he was a coward. Mary was shocked at the mocking descriptions of her husband wearing a Scottish kilt and cap as a disguise. She was even more disturbed by newspapers questioning her loyalty because of her ancestral ties to the South.

Many of Washington's leading socialites initially snubbed Mary. She responded by organizing a series of receptions, marine band concerts, and elegant formal levees that featured sumptuous spreads of food. Mary also delighted in following the latest fashion trends and had an Achilles' heel when it came to clothes. Rationalizing her fashion purchases as required by the demands of being first lady, Mary ran up large debts that she kept from her husband.

Most of the photographs of Mary Lincoln show her with flowers intertwined in her hair, reflecting the popular trend of the time. Mary's love for flowers can be seen in her frequent gifts to friends and associates of bouquets of flowers from the Executive Mansion greenhouse. Elizabeth Keckley, a former slave and a leading dressmaker in Washington, D.C., became Mary's favorite source for fashion apparel. The relationship was such that Mary began to confide in Keckley and to use her for errands and as an intermediary with people. Mrs. Mary Ann Cuthbert helped out as a seamstress and served as a dressing maid. Eventually Cuthbert was promoted to head housekeeper.

A great shock awaited Mary after Lincoln's inauguration on March 4, 1861. The Executive Mansion (what we now call the White House) had been neglected by previous administrations. Numerous souvenir hunters had cut pieces of fabric from furniture, carpets were worn and stained, and the walls and draperies near spittoons showed traces of poorly aimed tobacco juice. There was insufficient china in the pantry; several different patterns would be needed to accommodate the guests at a formal state dinner. Even the front door could not be locked because the only key had been lost years ago! Instead of reflecting the authority and dignity of a great republic, the Executive Mansion looked like a rundown boardinghouse. Abraham Lincoln understood the meaning of symbols, therefore he continued the construction of the Capitol dome to reflect the strength of the Union. Mary Lincoln believed it necessary to refurbish the Executive Mansion to display America at its best to foreign diplomats as well as average citizens.

Congress provided a $20,000 appropriation to correct the shabby and shopworn appearance of 1600 Pennsylvania Avenue. Traveling to the finest stores in Washington, D.C., New York, and Philadelphia, Mary purchased new furniture, elegantly patterned French wallpapers, plush floor coverings, Haviland porcelain, and Dorflinger crystal for 190 guests—more than enough for a state dinner in the Blue Room. She also bought handsome leather-bound volumes of her favorite writers and poets for the library. After all the expenses were totaled, she had exceeded the original appropriation by more than $6,800, effectively overspending the four-year appropriation in less than a year.

Overspending of government appropriations was not an uncommon occurrence—then or now. Lincoln exploded when he learned of the problem: "It never can have my approval—I'll pay it out of my own pocket first—it would stink in the nostrils of the American people to have it said that the President of the United States had approved a bill overrunning an appropriation of $20,000 for flub dubs for this damned old house, when the soldiers cannot have blankets." What made matters worse were efforts by Mary and others to hide the problem by engaging in a series of illegal and misguided acts. Relying upon the assistance of the White House gardener, John Watt, money was funneled to the first lady through the padding of expenses for groundskeeping and by a ghost payroll scheme. The $100 a month salary for Mrs. Watt, who performed no services, was given to Mrs. Lincoln. Furthermore, an adventurer named Henry Wikoff became a favorite of Mrs. Lincoln's and persuaded her to give him an advance look at Abraham Lincoln's Annual Message to Congress—what we now call the State of the Union message. Unbeknownst to Mary Lincoln, the leading Democratic newspaper, *The New York Herald*, maintained Wikoff on its payroll. That the opposition newspaper would publish Lincoln's remarks before they were delivered to members of Congress infuriated Republican leaders.

A House judiciary committee began an investigation that eventually led them to Watt and Wikoff's misdeeds. Lincoln immediately banned Wikoff from the White House, removing a major source of trouble. John Watt claimed to own incriminating correspondence that implicated Mary Lincoln; he demanded hush money, but supposedly relented when threatened with criminal proceedings. Orville Hickman Browning, a close friend of Lincoln's and a senator from Illinois, had a lengthy conversation with White House watchman Thomas Stackpole. Noting in his diary a summary of the conversation, Browning recorded that when Lincoln discovered the misdeeds, "he was very indignant and refunded what had been thus filched from the government out of his private purse." From that point on, Mary's expenditures of public funds were carefully scrutinized by Benjamin Brown French (the commissioner of public buildings) and by Lincoln, prompting Mary to complain that her husband was "almost a monomaniac on the subject of honesty." The Republican majority in Congress passed two supplemental appropriations to cover Mary Lincoln's cost overruns.

If Mary's public spending was held in check, her private spending became a tangled web of intrigue. Merchants read about Mrs. Lincoln's elegant gowns and fashionable events. Most were more than willing to court her business and often provided unsolicited incentives of shawls or gloves. Following the Watt/Wikoff affair, Mary felt a need to become more secretive about her personal expenditures. In a series of recently acquired telegrams, Mary Lincoln resorted to communicating with merchants using the pseudonym of her housekeeper, Mary Ann Cuthbert. While it is well established that Mary frequently used assumed names following her husband's assassination, these telegrams are the first evidence that she practiced it while he was alive. Most of the telegrams are both urgent in tone and cryptic in meaning. In one exchange with a New York City furrier, Mary wrote, "I cannot agree upon that price, for the furs. Mrs. Cuthbert." Frequently, Mary communicated with intermediaries attending to "business" that is unclear but suggests that she was settling accounts. The full extent of her indebtedness would be revealed only after her husband's death.

Black Dress worn by Mary Lincoln circa 1861.
(Abraham Lincoln Presidential Library and Museum)

Mrs. Lincoln wore this dress to Mathew Brady's photographic studio in 1861 and consented to have her image taken to fill the public demand for pictures of the President and First Lady.

Photograph cases of Mary, Abraham, and Willie Lincoln with locks of their hair.
(The Collection of Louise and Barry Taper)

A common practice in nineteenth-century America was to place locks of an individual's hair in a framed picture. These gutta-percha ambrotype cases contain albumen prints of Abraham, Mary, and Willie Lincoln along with locks of their hair.

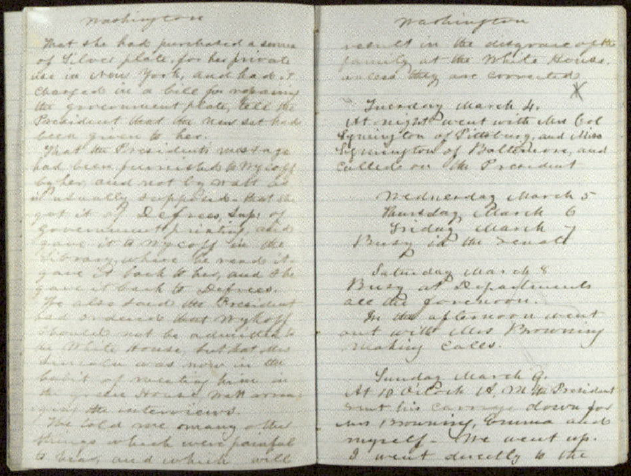

Washington

That she had purchased a service
of Silver plate, for her private
use in New York, and had it
charged in a bill for repairing
the government plate, tell the
President that the new set had
been given to her.
That the Presidents message
had been furnished to Wykoff
by her, and not by Watt as
is usually supposed - that she
got it of Defrees, Sup: of
government printing, and
gave it to Wykoff in the
Library, where he read it,
gave it back to her, and she
gave it back to Defrees.
She also said the President
had ordered that Wykoff
should not be admitted to
the White House, but that Mrs
Lincoln was now in the
habit of meeting him in
the green House [illegible] arran-
ging the interviews.
She told me many other
things which were painful
to hear, and which will

Washington

result in the disgrace of the
family at the White House,
unless they are corrected
X

Tuesday March 4.
At night went with Mrs Col
Symington of Pittsburg, and Miss
Symington of Baltimore, and
called on the President

Wednesday March 5
Thursday March 6
Friday March 7
Busy in the Senate

Saturday March 8
Busy at Departments
all the forenoon.
In the afternoon went
out with Mrs Browning
making calls.

Sunday March 9.
At 10 O'clock A.M. the President
sent his carriage down for
Mrs Browning, Emma and
myself - We went up.
I went directly to the

Orville Hickman Browning Diary.
(Abraham Lincoln Presidential Library and Museum)

In a number of entries, Browning relates conversations he had with various White House staff and Washington insiders providing less than flattering details about Mrs. Lincoln, especially her overspending.

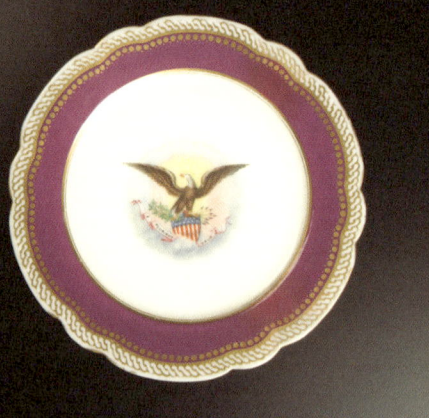

White House Official State China Plate.
(The Collection of Louise and Barry Taper)

A French Limoges porcelain purple dinner plate in the Solferino and gold pattern was selected by Mrs. Lincoln to serve as the official state china. Made by Haviland & Company, the pattern was also adopted by the Benjamin Harrison administration.

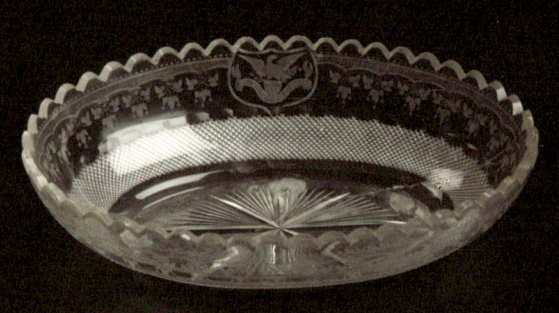

White House Crystal Relish Dish.
(The Collection of Louise and Barry Taper)

An American cut and engraved crystal relish dish was manufactured by the Dorflinger factory at the Greenpoint Glassworks, Brooklyn, New York, in 1861.

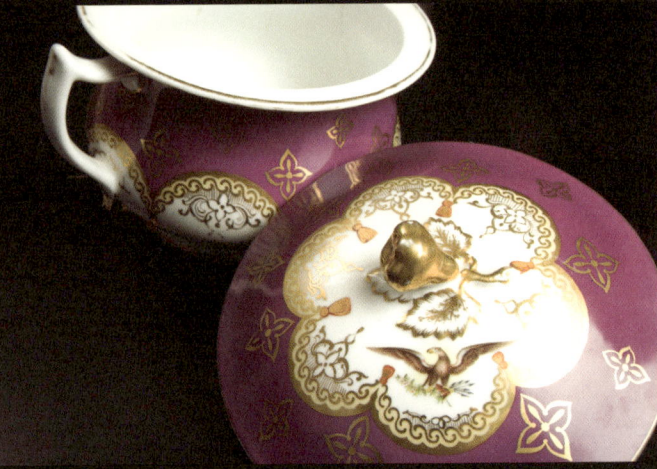

Personal Chamber Pot of Mary Lincoln.
(The Collection of Louise and Barry Taper)

Mrs. Lincoln used the same color scheme for the official state china as for her own chamber pot.

Presentation Bible.
(The Collection of Louise and Barry Taper)

Presented "To Mrs. President Lincoln from the Ladies of the First Methodist Episcopal Church, Lancaster City, Penna." on February 22, 1861, while she and president-elect Abraham Lincoln made their way to Washington, D.C.

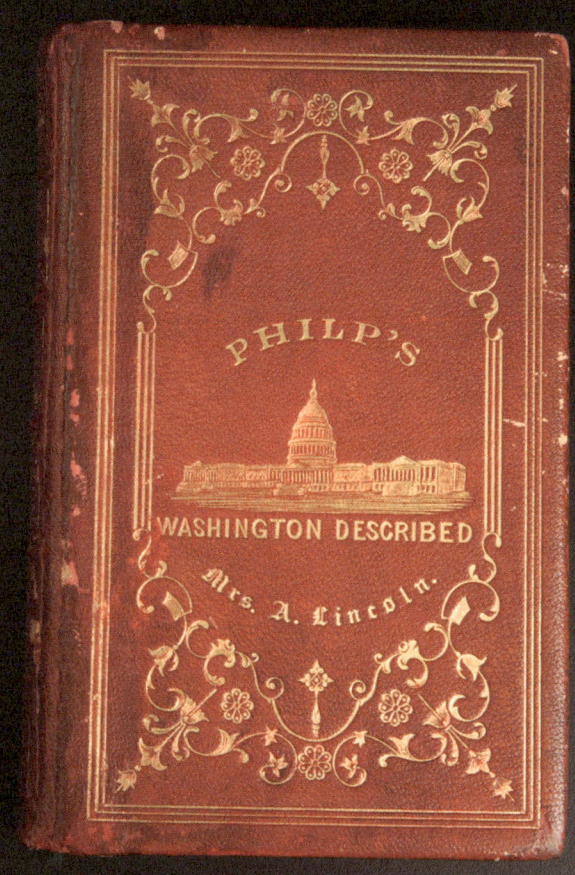

Gloves from Inaugural Ball.
(The Collection of Louise and Barry Taper)

A pair of white linen gloves with gold metal thread embroidery claimed to have been worn by Mrs. Lincoln at the First Inaugural Ball, 1861.

William D. Haley, *Philp's Washington Described*. A Complete View of the American Capital and the District of Columbia: with Many Notices, Historical, Topographical, and Scientific, of the Seat of Government. New York, 1861.
(The Collection of Louise and Barry Taper)

Mrs. Lincoln's personal copy with her name embossed in gilt on the cover of this popular guidebook of Washington, D.C.

FIRST LADY OF CONTROVERSY 35

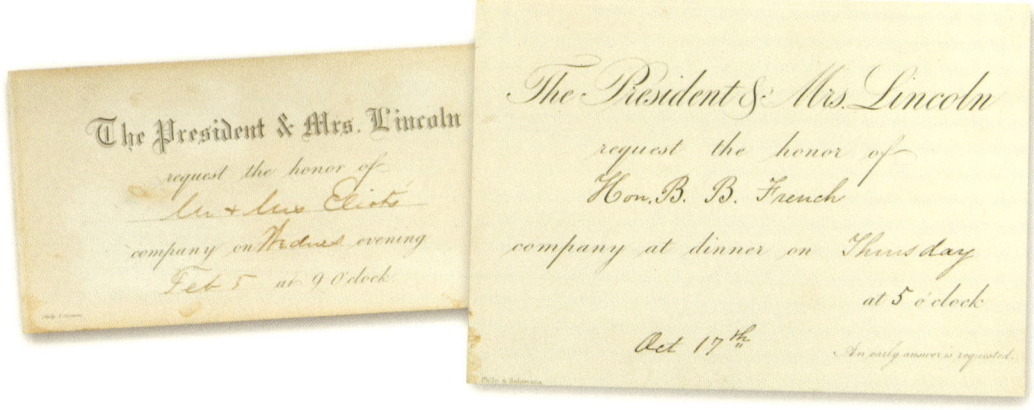

Presentation Cutlery Set Belonging to Henry Clay.
(Abraham Lincoln Presidential Library and Museum)

Thomas Clay, son of the illustrious Henry Clay, presented a cutlery set with the profile of the Great Compromiser engraved in the ivory handles at a private White House dinner on October 17, 1861.

Printed Invitations.
(The Collection of Louise and Barry Taper)

The verso side of the October 17, 1861, invitation to B.B. French, Commissioner of Public Buildings, contains the names of the other guests, including Thomas Clay. The February 5, 1862, reception for which Thomas Eliot, a Massachusetts Congressman, received this invitation was seen as a great social triumph for Mrs. Lincoln. Tragically, it was fifteen days following this event that Willie Lincoln died.

Diamond Pendant.
(Abraham Lincoln Presidential Library and Museum)

Given to Mrs. Lincoln by President Abraham Lincoln who, according to family lore, presented it with the utterance, "I give you my heart."

FIRST LADY OF CONTROVERSY 37

Lithograph of Lincoln Family.
(Abraham Lincoln Presidential Library and Museum)

CASUALTIES, CONTRABANDS, AND CARE

CASUALTIES, CONTRABANDS, AND CARE

The Civil War remains the bloodiest conflict in United States history. No one living at that time was unaffected by the loss of a loved one. Tragedy touched the Lincolns early in the war with the death of Elmer Ephraim Ellsworth. The young man studied law with Abraham Lincoln in Springfield, becoming a patent solicitor. He gained fame as a Zouave drill instructor, touring the country with the United States Zouave Cadets of Chicago in 1860. That same year he published the popular *Manual of Arms for Light Infantry*. Lincoln asked Ellsworth to accompany him to Washington in 1861, and he secured Ellsworth's appointment as a clerk in the War Department. When war broke out, Ellsworth went to New York City and organized a volunteer unit composed entirely of firemen—the famous 11th New York Volunteer Infantry or "Fire Zouaves." Ellsworth rushed the 1,110 men to Washington, D.C., on April 29, 1861, and Lincoln watched them sworn into service on May 5. The unit even extinguished a fire two days later.

The state of Virginia's withdrawal from the Union, on May 23, 1861, set in motion events that would cause the Lincolns personal grief. A rebel flag flying from a hotel in Alexandria, Virginia, was highly visible from the White House. On May 24, Ellsworth took his men across the Potomac River to take down the offending flag. James W. Jackson, the hotel's owner, shot and killed Ellsworth in the act of removing the rebel flag. The body was taken to the White House where it lay in state in the East Room. Both Abraham and Mary wept at the loss of the young man whom they had treated as a son.

There was more bad news. On October 22, 1861, news reached Washington that Colonel Edward Dickinson Baker had been killed in action at the Battle of Ball's Bluff. Baker and Lincoln shared experiences both in the Illinois legislature and in the legal profession. As Whigs, they each represented Illinois's Seventh Congressional District in Congress, and Abraham and Mary had named their late son Eddie after him. Baker's death undoubtedly brought back a flood of sad memories as President Lincoln attended the memorial service in the United States Senate.

Mary tried to keep spirits high and sent out 500 invitations for a White House ball to be held on February 5, 1862. Receiving an invitation was a prized honor, and many in Washington were trying to secure one. As the date approached, Willie became ill with a fever. Mary's immediate impulse was to cancel the event, but Abraham called in Dr. Robert Stone, who assured the first family that Willie was "in no immediate danger." The event on February 5 was a great social success. But Mary continued to worry about her son. According to Elizabeth Keckley, Mary excused herself to go "up-stairs several times, and stood by the bedside of the suffering boy." Shortly after the triumphant ball, Tad fell ill. Both boys were thought to have contracted typhoid fever. Mary exhausted herself by tending to their needs around the clock. Willie died at 5 p.m. on February 20, 1862. Lincoln visibly wept, and Mary became inconsolable, removing herself from public contact. Mary Jane Welles, the wife of Secretary of the Navy Gideon Welles, agreed to care for Tad, who remained ill but showed signs of recovery. Later, Dorothea Dix sent a nurse with experience tending soldiers with typhoid, Rebecca Pomroy, to replace Mrs. Welles.

Willie's body was embalmed and services were conducted in the Green Room of the White House. Abraham, Mary, and Robert paid their final respects in the Green Room before the casket was closed for the final time for the public funeral service in the East Room. Overcome with grief, Mary did not join the family when the casket was transported to Oak Hill Cemetery in Georgetown, where it was placed in a vault, awaiting the Lincolns' return to Springfield, Illinois. Mary came to believe that Willie's death resulted from the sin of pride. "I had become, so wrapped up in the world, so devoted to our own political advancement," Mary claimed, "that I thought of little else." The loss was not hers alone. Abraham struggled with the huge emptiness created by Willie's death. Lincoln overcame his grief by immersing himself even more deeply in work. Mary, however, struggled with her sense of loss. The traditional Christian beliefs of a peaceful heavenly afterlife no longer provided comfort. Elizabeth Keckley suggested that Mary try spiritualism, in which one communicated with a departed loved one through a medium. A number of seances were held in the White House and, at times, Mary felt Willie's presence. Noah Brooks, a journalist and friend of the Lincolns, claimed that the president attended a few of the seances to make certain a charlatan did not swindle Mary. Brooks vividly describes his unmasking of one popular medium, Lord Colchester, who presided over one of Mary's gatherings.

On September 24, 1863, Lincoln sent Mary, who was in New York City, a telegram describing the terrible Union defeat at Chickamauga. Included in the telegram was news that Mary's brother-in-law, Brigadier General Benjamin Hardin Helm, had died in the battle. Both the Lincolns were close to Mary's half-sister Emilie Todd and Benjamin, a graduate of West Point. Emilie had her husband buried in Atlanta, Georgia, and then sought to rejoin her family in Lexington, Kentucky. Lincoln wrote out an order to allow Emilie to pass through Union lines. Because she refused to take the prescribed loyalty oath, she and her daughter Katherine were detained at Fortress Monroe. Lincoln ordered them to be sent to him at the White House. The Lincolns enjoyed being reunited with Emilie and Katherine, but the time was not entirely pleasant, with newspapers accusing the Lincolns of harboring a Southern spy in the Executive Mansion. Eventually, Emilie and Katherine Helm made it back to Lexington on December 20, 1864.

As casualties mounted, the public questioned why Robert Lincoln was not in uniform. His graduation from Harvard in 1864 fed further speculation that he would enlist. Mary opposed Robert's plan, refusing to have any more of her sons die while she lived. Acceding to his mother's wishes, Robert enrolled in law school. Lincoln was well aware of the demands of public opinion. As president, Lincoln set an example by paying $300 for a substitute for himself. Serving in the army for Lincoln was John Summerfield Staples of Stroudsburg, Pennsylvania. But Robert did not want a substitute, and Mary did not want her son in danger. Lincoln resolved the matter by writing a personal letter to Ulysses Grant, urging him to "Please read and answer this letter as though I was not President, but only a friend . . . Could he [Robert], without embarrassment to you, or detriment to the service, go into your Military family with some nominal rank, I, and not the public, furnishing his necessary means?" Two days later Grant replied that he would be happy to have Robert serve on his staff with the rank of captain.

The realities of the war continued to serve as a grim reminder to the many human needs that required attention. Mary's grief was eventually overcome by the realization of the pain of others. Elizabeth Keckley apprised her of the growing population of black refugees from slavery. These refugees were commonly referred to as "contrabands." Until emancipation was a formalized policy, Union generals justified the liberation of slaves as nothing more than depriving Southerners of their human "property." Contraband populations in Washington, D.C., grew from 400 in April 1862 to over 5,000 by year's end. At the end of the war, 40,000 freed blacks had settled in Washington, D.C. Keckley played a prominent role among blacks in the city to organize the Contraband Relief Association.

Mary wrote to her husband an impassioned request on November 3, 1862, indicating that contrabands in Washington "are suffering intensely, many without bed covering & having to use any bits of carpeting to cover themselves—Many dying of want." She requested that her husband send $200 from a special fund to the Contraband Relief Association because "the cause of humanity requires it." In spite of Mary's efforts to enlist white support for the cause, funds were largely raised from blacks by Keckley and others. The president and first lady frequently distributed food and other goods to former slaves in a large contraband camp on the road to the Soldier's Home where the Lincoln family spent its summers.

Other signs of Mary's reengagement with life were her frequent appearances at many of Washington's army hospitals. Soldier accounts of her are overwhelmingly positive, reflecting the social grace and education of her youth. Her hospital visits consisted of what was required at the moment. She would often bring food from the kitchen or flowers from the conservatory and distribute them among the soldiers. Often, soldiers who were illiterate or had an arm amputated would ask her to pen a letter for them to loved ones. Her task during these visits was to serve the needs of the soldiers, whatever that might require. These visits were not for the faint of heart, given the overwhelming sight of mangled bodies and the smell of sickness and death that was ever-present. William O. Stoddard, who served as a secretary to Lincoln, occasionally accompanied Mary on these hospital excursions. He believed that "If she [Mary Lincoln] had been worldly-wise, she would have carried with her newspaper correspondents of both sexes every time she went, and she would have them take shorthand notes of what she said to the sick soldiers, and of what the sick soldiers said to her." Perhaps Mary understood that these genuine acts of kindness were best kept secret.

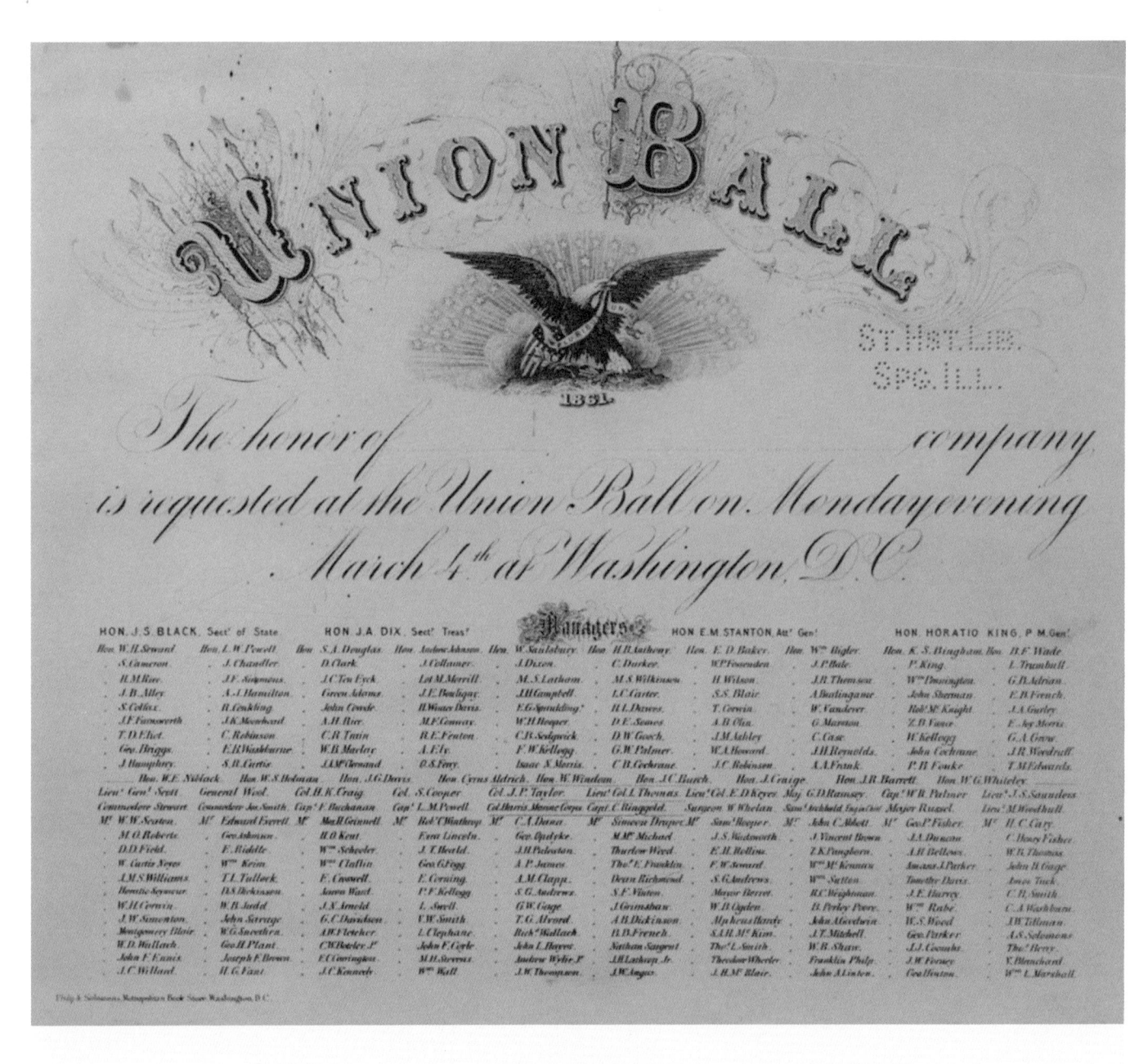

Union Ball Invitation, 1861.
(Abraham Lincoln Presidential Library and Museum)

Lincoln's inaugural ball on March 4, 1861, took place in an armed capital city amid rumors of Presidential assassination and Southern invasion. The newspapers called this event a "brilliant occasion."

> Soldiers Home.
>
> Please accept this bouquet from the W. House garden
>
> My Dear Mrs Brayman,
>
> I am feeling sadly, the effects of my sunny rides, several days last week, & will be unable to venture in the city to day, yet by remaining quiet, will hope to have the pleasure of seeing you tomorrow morning & have you drive with me.
>
> Sincerely yrs Mary Lincoln

Mary Lincoln, autograph letter signed,
to Mary Brayman, circa Spring 1862.
(The Collection of Louise and Barry Taper)

Writing to an old Springfield friend shortly after Willie's death, Mary relates how her continuing grief prevents her from venturing into "the city today." Mrs. Lincoln offers Brayman a bouquet from the White House garden.

Mary Lincoln, autograph letter signed,
to Elizabeth Keckley, November 22, 1864.
(The Collection of Louise and Barry Taper)

Sending a note through the military telegraph office, Mrs. Lincoln informs Keckley that a check has been sent for the purchase of articles. She also requests Keckley to "leave the goods with Mrs. Martin."

Abraham Lincoln, autograph telegram signed, to Mary Lincoln, Sept. 24, 1863, informing her of the death of her brother-in-law, Confederate Brig. Gen. Ben Helm, at the battle of Chickamauga, Georgia.
(Abraham Lincoln Presidential Library and Museum)

Notes by both Lincolns and two officials, May 1864,
showing the affectionate term "Mother" and both
parents' efforts to please Tad.
(The Collection of Louise and Barry Taper)

FUNERAL ADDRESS

DELIVERED BY

REV. DR. GURLEY,

ON THE OCCASION OF THE

DEATH OF WILLIAM WALLACE LINCOLN.

FEBRUARY 24, 1862.

SAD and solemn is the occasion that brings us here to-day. A dark shadow of affliction has suddenly fallen upon this habitation, and upon the hearts of its inmates. The news thereof has already gone forth to the extremities of the country.

The Nation has heard it with deep and tender emotions. The eye of the Nation is moistened with tears, as it turns to-day to the Presidential Mansion; the heart of the Nation sympathizes with its Chief Magistrate, while to the unprecedented weight of civil care which presses upon him is added the burden of this great domestic sorrow; and the prayer of the Nation ascends to Heaven on his behalf, and on the behalf of his weeping family, that God's grace may be sufficient for them, and that in this hour of sore bereavement and trial, they may have the presence and succor of Him, who has said, "Come unto me all ye that labor and are heavy laden, and I will give you rest."

64993

Funeral Address on death of Willie Lincoln,
February 24, 1862.
(Abraham Lincoln Presidential Library and Museum)

Willie's death from typhoid at age 11 may have permanently affected his mother's emotions and thoughts.

Photograph of Mary Lincoln, possibly
by William H. Mumler, circa 1865.
(Abraham Lincoln Presidential Library and Museum)

"CRUSHING THIS TERRIBLE REBELLION"

"CRUSHING THIS TERRIBLE REBELLION"

The war exacted a heavy toll on the Lincolns. Mary witnessed her husband become so overwhelmed by work that he grew thin from skipping meals. She insisted that he eat breakfast with her, often inviting friends over to force him into joining her at the table. She also instituted an afternoon carriage ride to give him a break from the concerns of the war and the press of visitors requesting a few minutes of the president's time. Whenever possible, trips to the opera and theater served as good diversions, since they both enjoyed the performing arts. It may have appeared frivolous to an outside observer, but such entertainment provided necessary distraction and leaven to a world-weary president.

Like much of the North, Mary rejoiced at her husband's reelection. She had always protected him from enemies, real and perceived. Her rants against cabinet members and political associates who struck her as disloyal and untrustworthy were quietly noted by the president, who did not need any more enemies but rather practical accommodation with those who disagreed with his policies. As Lincoln urged the nation to "strive on to finish the work we are in," a sense of anticipation that the war would soon end was in the forefront of the public mind. On March 10, 1865, Mary Lincoln invited Iowa Senator James Harlan and his wife and daughter to join the Lincolns to see the opera "The Jewess." Robert had taken their daughter Mary to the inaugural ball, and rumors circulated that a wedding was on the horizon. His time away from the war was brief—just long enough to see his father take the oath of office for a second term. Robert quickly returned to duty.

Two weeks following Lincoln's second inaugural, General Grant invited the president to visit him at City Point, Virginia, located on the James River. The President and Mrs. Lincoln traveled to Grant's headquarters on the steamship *River Queen*. Lincoln met numerous times in closed-door sessions with Grant and joined him at such public events as reviewing the troops. Mary was ill-tempered, in part because of a migraine and also from a feeling of being neglected. Arriving late to the review of troops, Mary witnessed her husband riding alongside the very attractive Mrs. Ord. Jealousy got the better of her, and Mary verbally exploded at Mrs. Ord and her husband. One observer recalled Lincoln bearing the rant "as Christ might have done, with an expression of pain and sadness that cut one to the heart, but with supreme calmness and dignity."

On April 9, 1865, Robert E. Lee surrendered to Grant at Appomattox Courthouse in Virginia. Robert Todd Lincoln was present to witness the historic occasion. Although other active Confederate armies remained intact, Lee represented the symbolic heart of the Confederate military force. His defeat marked the end of the Confederacy. The celebrations in Washington and throughout the North were spontaneous and continuous. Mary wrote to newspaper editor James Gordon Bennett expressing her joy over the surrender and thanking him for his "devotion to our cause and great influence exerted in crushing, this terrible rebellion."

On April 14, 1865, the Lincolns took their afternoon carriage ride, talking about the future and possible travel. Laura Keene's theatrical troupe planned a benefit performance of a British comedy of manners, "Our American Cousin." Flyers announcing the Lincolns' attendance promised a sold-out performance. What began as an enjoyable evening out ended in tragedy when John Wilkes Booth, bitter from the defeat of the Confederacy, shot Lincoln as he watched the play.

Mary caught her husband as he slumped forward. There was confusion in the box, with Booth and Major Henry Rathbone, one of the Lincolns' guests, fighting. Blood spewed from Rathbone's arm where Booth stabbed him and merged with the blood slowly oozing from Lincoln's head. Commotion followed as military surgeons tried to obtain access to the presidential box to attend to the wounded men. Mary followed the transport of her husband's body across the street to the Petersen House. Her sobbings so irritated Secretary of War Edwin Stanton that he had her removed from the room. About six in the morning Mary Lincoln went to see and kiss her dying husband one last time. Robert escorted her back to the White House, where Elizabeth Keckley took over her care. There is no record that Mary took part in any of the public services at the White House or in Washington, her grief being so great. Yet, the Cuthbert telegrams reveal that two days following her husband's death, she was still trying to resolve various undisclosed business matters. In times of great stress, it is not unusual for people to focus on immediate, obtainable goals. The telegrams reveal that Mary continued to interact with the outside world within the bounds of her own economic interest. Her husband was dead but her creditors were not. That fact forced her to confront life, even as she often claimed that she wished she were dead.

**Mary Lincoln, autograph letter signed,
to Ann Eliza Harlan, March 10, 1865.**
(The Collection of Louise and Barry Taper)

President and Mrs. Lincoln invite Senator, Mrs.,
and their daughter Mary Harlan to the opera.
Mary Harlan would later marry Robert Lincoln.

**Mary Lincoln, autograph letter signed,
to Abram Wakeman, January 30, 1865.**
(The Collection of Louise and Barry Taper)

Mary invites Wakeman, a New York lawyer, to the theatre.
Commenting that she and the President had "quite a little
laugh together…not withstanding our opposite natures,
our lives have been eminently peaceful."

**Mary Lincoln, autograph letter signed,
to James Gordon Bennett, April 13, 1865.**
(The Collection of Louise and Barry Taper)

Writing the day prior to Abraham Lincoln's assassination,
Mary tells the New York publisher, "we are rejoicing beyond expression,
over our great & glorious victories & appreciate…your devotion to our
cause & great influence…in crushing this terrible rebellion."

**Abraham Lincoln, autograph letter signed,
to Solomon Foote, 1863.**
(The Collection of Louise and Barry Taper)

Lincoln indicates that the invitation to Foote to accompany
them to the opera was at the request of "Mrs. L." This was part
of Mary's ongoing attempts to give her husband diversions
from the press of official duties.

Abraham Lincoln, autograph note signed,
to Mrs. William W. Morris, March 28, 1864.
(The Collection of Louise and Barry Taper)

The President acts as his wife's social secretary by writing this note: "Mrs. L. is confined to her room by illness but is improving & writes now she can see Mrs. Morris at 1 o'clock to-morrow."

Gideon Welles, autograph telegram signed,
to Jacob Zeilin, February 8, 1865.
(The Collection of Louise and Barry Taper)

The Secretary of the Navy informs the Commander of the Marine Corps band that "Mrs. Lincoln desires nine or ten pieces of music at seven o'clock this evening. She gives a dinner party."

Piece from dress worn by Mrs. Lincoln
to Ford's Theatre, April 14, 1865.
(The Collection of Louise and Barry Taper)

According to some accounts, Mrs. Lincoln gave the dress to Mrs. Slade, the wife of White House valet William Slade. The dress has never been located but many souvenir pieces exist.

FIRST LADY OF CONTROVERSY 55

Blood-stained fan of Mary Lincoln's from Ford's Theatre, April 14, 1865.
(The Collection of Louise and Barry Taper)

This ivory and white silk hand fan was used by Mary Lincoln at Ford's
Theatre and remained a grim reminder of that tragic evening.

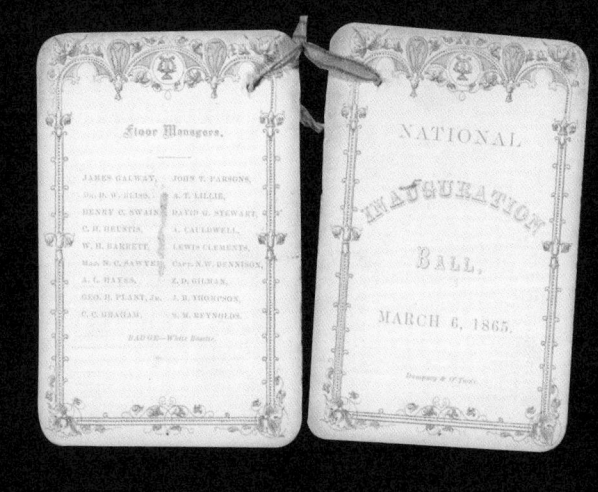

Second Inaugural Ball Dance Program and Menu, March 6, 1865.
(The Collection of Louise and Barry Taper)

The printed dance program and sumptuous Bill of Fare menu reflect the celebrations surrounding Lincoln's second inaugural. He was the first president since Andrew Jackson (1829-1837) to be elected to a second term.

FIRST LADY OF CONTROVERSY 57

> Mr John Kerr
> China Hall
> Chesnut Street
> Philadelphia
>
> The Madame would like to see you Or here immediately
>
> Mrs Cuthbert

Mrs. Cuthbert [Mary Lincoln], autograph telegram signed, to Mr. James K. Kerr, May 18, 1865.
(Abraham Lincoln Presidential Library and Museum)

One of numerous telegrams of Mary Lincoln to merchants using the pseudonym 'Mrs. Cuthbert.' In this telegram, Mary mistakenly refers to James Kerr as "John" but indicates that "Madame would like to see you are here immediately."

"THE INTENSE GRIEF I NOW ENDURE"

"THE INTENSE GRIEF I NOW ENDURE"

May 23 and 24, 1865, were designated for celebration as corps from the Army of the Potomac and the Army of the Cumberland marched in review past President Andrew Johnson and General Ulysses S. Grant. While Washington celebrated, Mary Lincoln quietly departed the White House and boarded a train for Chicago. The realities of her husband's death were being brought into sharper focus with each passing day. Lincoln had not planned for his death, leaving no will to instruct his heirs. Judge David Davis, who rode the Eighth Judicial Circuit in Illinois with Lincoln, was asked to serve as administrator of the estate. Unlike today, when the surviving spouse would inherit the estate, Davis was obligated by law to divide the estate into three equal portions for each of the surviving family members: Mary, Robert, and Tad. Because Tad Lincoln was a minor, a guardian needed to be appointed to protect his interests. Robert Lincoln assumed the responsibility temporarily and eventually turned it over to Davis once the estate was settled. It took Davis two years to collect all the outstanding debts and bills presented against the estate. By November 1867 Lincoln's three survivors had received more than $36,000 each.

Mary struggled with her emotions. She was painfully aware of the gifts being offered to the heroes of the war, particularly Ulysses S. Grant who was given homes in Washington, D.C., Galena, Illinois, and Philadelphia, Pennsylvania, by grateful citizens. Mary hoped that as the widow of the martyred president, she would be provided for in similar fashion. Horace Greeley, the mercurial editor of the *New York Tribune,* began a campaign to raise $100,000 as a pension for Mrs. Lincoln, asking readers to each contribute one dollar. At the same time Josiah G. Holland, editor of the Springfield, Massachusetts *Republican*, began interviewing Lincoln's associates in Springfield, Illinois, with plans to write a biography of the sixteenth president. Returning home, Holland wrote, "It has been ascertained that the late President left an ample fortune—very much larger than first supposed." By June, petition papers filed by the estate were made public, revealing an estimated value of $75,000. That coupled with rumors of Mary's shopping sprees as first lady and several efforts to raise money for monuments to Lincoln—including the National Lincoln Monument Association's efforts to construct the Lincoln Tomb in Springfield—effectively ended private efforts to provide financial relief to Mary.

Public efforts continued, as did Mary's own efforts to obtain her husband's salary. She believed the government rightly owed her the remaining four years of salary that her husband would have earned as president, approximately $100,000 ($25,000 per year). Getting Congress to give her the salary for 1865 proved difficult enough. Mary was tireless in writing letters and having people intercede for her in Washington. By December, she learned that Congress had passed a law granting her the salary for 1865. Even then the final amount provided only $22,025—the full year's salary minus six weeks of pay Lincoln received in his second term and federal taxes. The money paid off all outstanding debts, with the remainder placed into government bonds.

Mary's income until the estate was settled amounted to $1,500 annually. After a brief week's stay in Chicago at the fashionable Tremont House, Mary and her sons relocated to the Hyde Park Hotel and then, after a number of months, to the Clifton House on the corner of Wabash and Madison streets. Her desire for homeownership was realized with the help of Simon Cameron, a Pennsylvania politician and former secretary of war. Using money provided by Cameron, Mary purchased a house at 375 West Washington Street in Chicago. But Mary found it hard to make ends meet, and by May 1867 she had moved out, using it as a rental property to increase her own income by $500 annually.

Tad was enrolled at Brown School and later at the Chicago Academy. Mary took Tad to a dentist, who fitted him with a spring-framed device to improve his speech. But Robert concluded that the device had the opposite effect, making Tad's speech incomprehensible. Instead, an elocution expert at the Chicago Academy, Professor Amasa McCoy, worked with Tad in vastly improving his diction.

Robert finished his study of law with the firm of Scammon, McCagg and Fuller, and took additional courses at the University of Chicago. He obtained his law license on February 25, 1867, and quickly set up a partnership with Charles T. Scammon, whose father was the principal in the firm. Robert discovered his partner had a drinking problem and ended the business relationship. While he worked hard for business, Robert discovered that his name provided many business advantages. But even the name of Lincoln could not overcome two embarrassing events.

The first occurred on November 16, 1866, at a public lecture in Springfield, Illinois. William Henry Herndon, Abraham Lincoln's law partner, had been collecting materials for a biography and delivering public lectures on Lincoln. On this night, he presented "A. Lincoln—Miss Ann Rutledge, New Salem—Pioneering, and the poem called 'Immortality'—or 'Oh Why Should the Spirit of Mortal Be Proud,'" in which he claimed that Lincoln loved Ann Rutledge and only Ann Rutledge. The lecture offended Robert, who wrote to David Davis, "Mr. William H. Herndon is making an ass of himself." Mary was less generous in her remarks when she obtained a copy in March of 1867. Claiming Herndon was "a hopeless inebriate" and "a dirty dog," Mary refused to concede any legitimacy to the claim of a loveless marriage, declaring "Ann Rutledge, is a myth." As one biographer noted, "from then on it was open warfare" between Mary and Herndon.

The other incident, frequently identified as "The Old Clothes Scandal," occurred in the fall of 1867. Obsessed with the state of her financial affairs, Mary enlisted the help of Elizabeth Keckley to explore the possible sale of her jewelry, gowns, shawls, and other fashion accessories to New York agents. Assuming the name "Mrs. Clarke," Mary and Keckley stayed at the St. Denis Hotel. Mary hid her face behind a black mourning veil and paid a visit to W. H. Brady & Company, a diamond broker on Broadway. Inspecting the jewelry she brought, they discovered Mary Lincoln's name engraved inside one of the rings.

Samuel Keyes, Brady's partner, met Mary at the hotel and promised that her items could bring as much as $100,000. But the catch was that she needed to supply them with letters that they could take to political figures whom President Lincoln had appointed to office. They argued that these politicians would not want it known that they turned down assisting Mrs. Lincoln in her hour of need. Mary wrote the letters, but the politicians were not interested in being blackmailed, and few of the clothes sold. Brady and Keyes then placed Mary's wardrobe on exhibition and arranged to have the letters published in the leading Democratic newspaper, the *New York World.* Soon editors and newspapers across the country began to weigh in with their own opinions, mocking the condition of the clothes, accusing Mary of being greedy and vulgar, and dredging up old partisan complaints of corruption in

Lincoln's administration. The most damaging accusations that appeared in print were claims that she was insane. Mary, deeply embarrassed by the public furor, asked for her clothes back. Brady and Keyes sent her a bill for $824, which she paid.

But there was a bright spot when Robert announced his plans to wed Mary Harlan. On September 24, 1868, a small gathering of family and close friends witnessed the marriage at the Washington, D.C., residence of Senator James Harlan. Mary Lincoln considered the marriage " a great gain" and claimed "I have known and loved" Mary Harlan "since her childhood." Indeed, Robert's marriage "is the only sunbeam in my sad future," Mary intimated to a friend. On October 1, 1868, Mary and Tad boarded the steamer *City of Baltimore* and fled the country for Europe.

Mary Lincoln's Mourning Jewelry.
(The Collection of Louise and Barry Taper)

Consisting of carved onyx disks with black enamel and yellow gold, this pin matches a pair of ear pendants and was used by Mrs. Lincoln following the death of her husband.

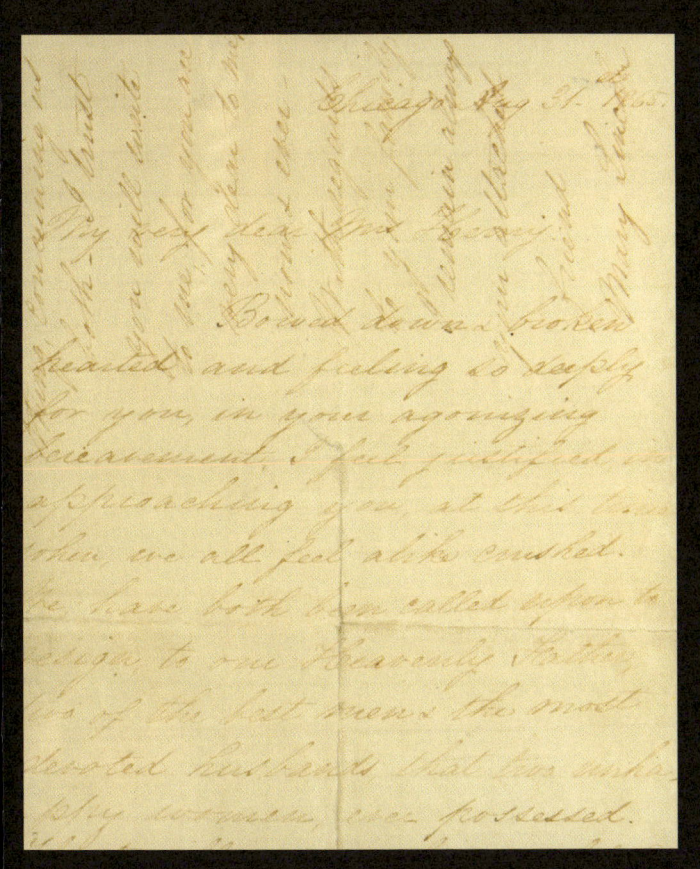

Mary Lincoln, autograph letter signed,
to Eliza Henry, August 31, 1865.
(The Collection of Louise and Barry Taper)

Mary writes to console the wife of family friend
Anson G. Henry who drowned recently.
In it Mary admits, "I long to lay my own weary head,
down to rest, by the side of my darling husband…."

Mary Lincoln, autograph letter signed,
to Francis E. Spinner, January 11, 1866.
(The Collection of Louise and Barry Taper)

This letter is part of a series of letters between Mary and
the United States Treasurer concerning the dispensation of
President Lincoln's remaining salary for 1865. Congress
eventually voted to grant Mary the remaining $22,000, as
represented by The Adams Express Company check.

FIRST LADY OF CONTROVERSY 65

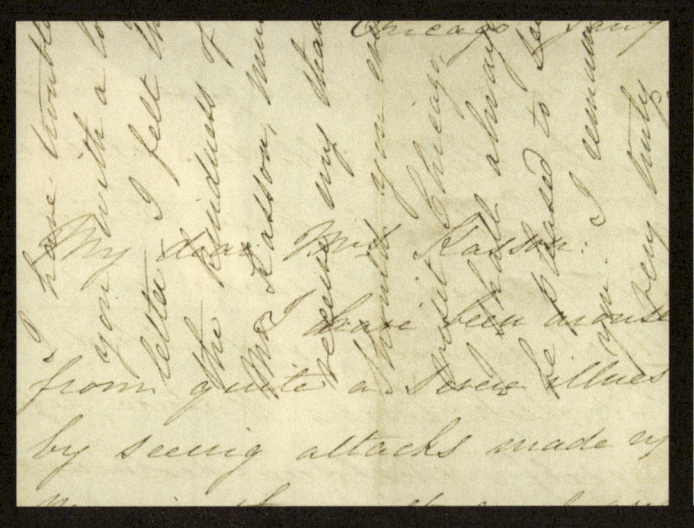

**Mary Lincoln, autograph letter signed,
to Caroline Kasson, January 20, 1866.**
(The Collection of Louise and Barry Taper)

This letter to a Chicago friend denies charges raised by newspapers that she took furniture and other government property from the White House. Mary also reasserts her grief, claiming "My beloved husband was my all, I almost worshipped him & his deep, loving nature…"

**Mary Lincoln, autograph letter signed,
to Benjamin Richardson, June 16, 1868.**
(The Collection of Louise and Barry Taper)

Benjamin Richardson was an eccentric collector who had been seeking artifacts of Abraham Lincoln from Mary. In this letter, Mary accommodates him by sending the blood-stained gloves and handkerchief from Ford's Theatre. She was frequently asked for such things throughout her life.

**Mary Lincoln, autograph letter signed,
to Martha Stafford, July 18, 1868.**
(The Collection of Louise and Barry Taper)

As Mary prepared to leave for Europe with Tad, they spent time at a health resort in Cresson Springs, Pennsylvania. Writing to a housekeeper at the Clifton House where she resided, Mary asks for a box of hair braids to be forwarded to her. She also states that "Tad has met some fine boys here & looks very happy."

**Mary Lincoln, autograph letter signed,
to Jesse Kilgore Dubois, July 26, 1868.**
(The Collection of Louise and Barry Taper)

Dubois was a director with the National Lincoln Monument Association, the group responsible for constructing the Lincoln Tomb. Mary asks about progress on the vault. She also notes that "Robert, grows every day more and more like his father…"

Mary Lincoln, autograph letter signed,
to Eliza Slataper, September 21, 1868.
(The Collection of Louise and Barry Taper)

At the Cresson Springs spa, Mary struck up a friendship with
Eliza Slataper, wife a successful civil engineer from Pittsburgh. Mary
recalls Slataper's kindness toward Tad when he lost his pocket change.

Mary Lincoln, autograph letter signed,
to Eliza Slataper, September 25, 1868.
(The Collection of Louise and Barry Taper)

Recounting the recent marriage of her son Robert to Mary Harlan,
the daughter of Iowa Senator James Harlan, Mary writes
"The marriage…passed off finely…no more than 30 persons
present…very elegant presents given."

Robert T. Lincoln and
Mary Harlan Lincoln
Marriage License,
September 24, 1868.
(The Collection of Louise and Barry Taper)

FIRST LADY OF CONTROVERSY 67

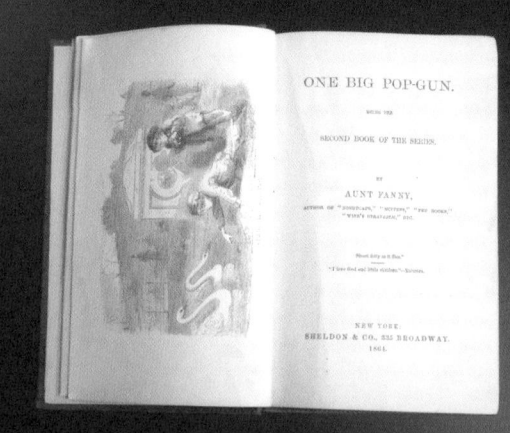

Aunt Fanny [Frances Barrow], *One Big Pop-Gun*, New York: Sheldon & Co., 1864.
(The Collection of Louise and Barry Taper)

A popular children's author, Frances Barrow dedicated all of the books in this series to Tad. Mary sent Barrow a thank-you note and commented that "My little boy's name is Thomas Lincoln, a very plain name…"

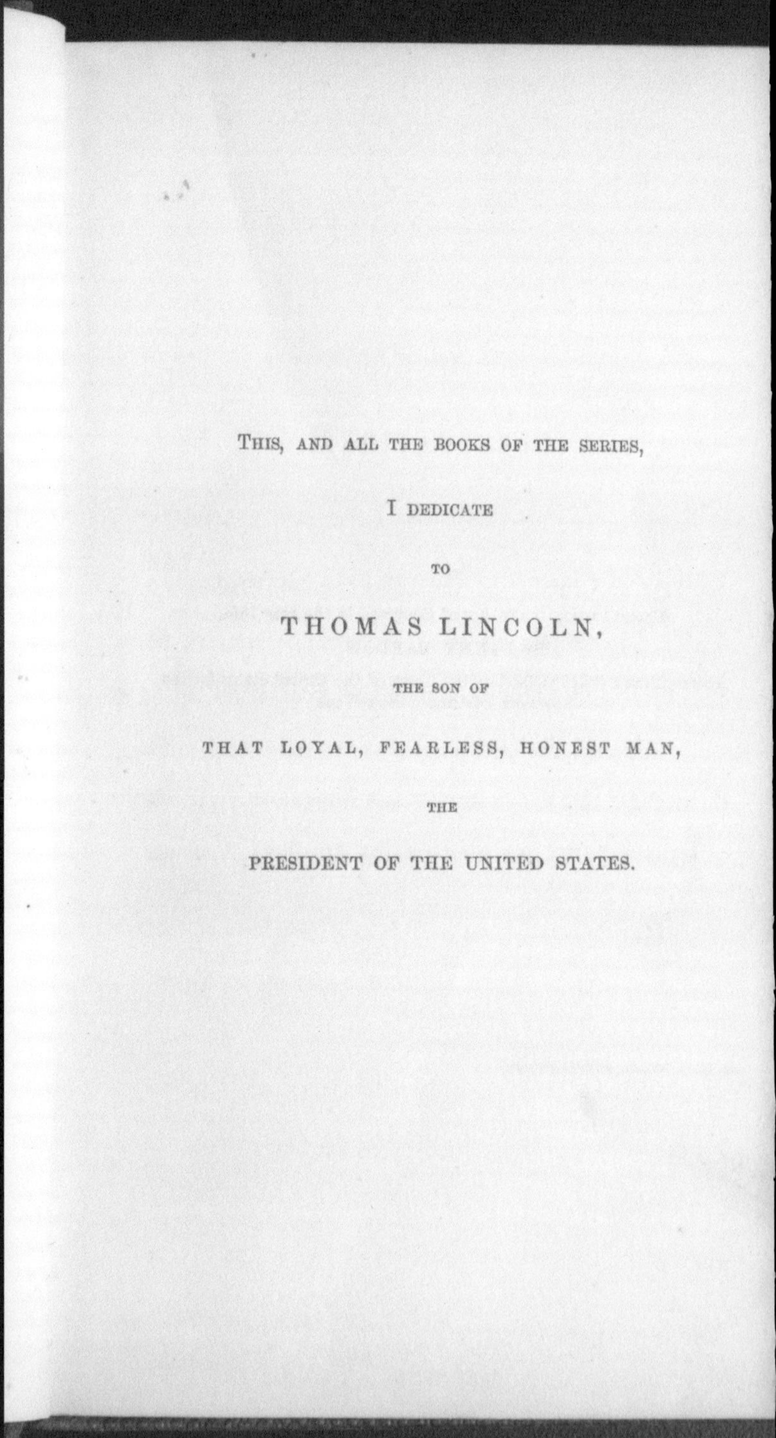

This, and all the books of the series,

I dedicate

to

THOMAS LINCOLN,

the son of

that loyal, fearless, honest man,

the

PRESIDENT OF THE UNITED STATES.

China bowl.
(Abraham Lincoln Presidential Library and Museum)
This pattern was used in Chicago by Mary and Tad Lincoln.

Photograph of Mary Lincoln, probably by E. & H. T. Anthony Company, circa autumn 1863.
(Abraham Lincoln Presidential Library and Museum)

AMERICANS ABROAD

AMERICANS ABROAD

The *City of Baltimore* made the transatlantic voyage in twelve days. It encountered one serious storm, but the remainder of the trip was uneventful. Docking in Bremen, Germany, Mary and Tad proceeded to Frankfurt, on the Main River. Frankfurt was an elegant old city with a vibrant group of English-speaking expatriates. Staying at the comfortable Hotel Angleterre, Mary found the new setting a welcome change from America. She encountered numerous Americans, including Henry Mason, who made a fortune manufacturing organs, Robert Allen, whom she knew from Springfield, Illinois, and Sally Orne, wife of a wealthy carpet manufacturer and old friend from Washington, D.C. Mary used her time in Europe to visit the spas and health resorts in Germany, France, Italy, Austria, and England.

Tad was enrolled in Dr. Hohagen's Institute, a boarding school in Frankfurt. Catering to wealthy sons of the expatriates, the school helped Tad overcome his previous educational deficiencies. When Mary took Tad on her excursions to Scotland and England, a tutor was secured to continue his training. All in all, Tad's education abroad produced remarkable results.

A pleasant note from the Reverend James Smith in 1869 invited Mary and Tad to visit him in Scotland. No doubt Mary recalled Smith's comforting words following Eddie's death. Lincoln had appointed Smith's son to serve as the American consul at Dundee, Scotland, and upon his son's resignation, Smith himself was given the position. Believing that the summer of 1869 might be his last, he wished to see Mrs. Lincoln one last time. The invitation allowed Mary to visit the ancestral homeland of the Todds as well as to see the birthplace of Robert Burns and Balmoral Castle.

The expense of living abroad turned out to be greater than anticipated. Sally Orne's brother, Charles O'Neill, a congressman from Pennsylvania, began to push for a government pension for Mary. Senator Charles Sumner was also a strong advocate for the measure. He began efforts as early as 1868, but the legislation kept languishing in committee. The debate in the Senate was colored by accusations of disloyalty. Vermont senator Justin Morrill, upset that Mrs. Lincoln resided abroad, believed that Tad "had much better be educated here at home under American institutions than to be educated abroad, where he will not grow up in the principles of his father." Ultimately, both the House and Senate voted Mary Lincoln a $3,000 annual pension. President Grant signed the bill on July 15, 1870, thus ending Mary's obsession with money.

In the summer of 1870, the Franco-Prussian War erupted. General Philip Sheridan traveled to Europe to witness the conflict, and he took the opportunity to call upon Mrs. Lincoln. Sheridan then followed the German army into Paris. Mary began seriously considering a return to America. In the fall of 1870, she and Tad relocated to England. Mary spent a good deal of time at the mineral baths of Leamington, a town 100 miles northwest of London. After reviving her health and her spirits, she resided in London, making occasional side trips on the continent. Suffering from ill-health throughout the winter of 1870 and desiring to see a granddaughter named after her who had been born to Robert and Mary a year earlier, Mary and Tad Lincoln boarded the Cunard liner *Russia* in Liverpool on April 29, 1871, to head to New York City.

Undergarments of Mary Lincoln.
(The Collection of Louise and Barry Taper)

This ensemble consists of a camisole top and a bloomers slip bottom. It is hand-stitched cotton with the original draw-string ribbon.

Night Cap of Mary Lincoln.
(The Collection of Louise and Barry Taper)

This linen night cap has a pleated crest and back with a ruffled frill.

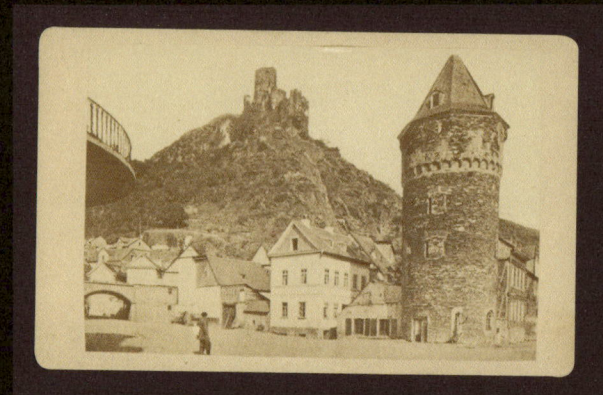

Carte-de-visite of a German Castle.
(Abraham Lincoln Presidential Library and Museum)

Throughout her European travels, Mary purchased small photographic cards known as cartes-de-visite and kept them in an album. Many show old castles such as this scene.

Music box.
(Abraham Lincoln Presidential Library and Museum)

This music box could date as early as the Springfield years but may have been obtained in the Lincoln presidency. It plays an assortment of operatic arias, reflecting the Lincolns' love of music.

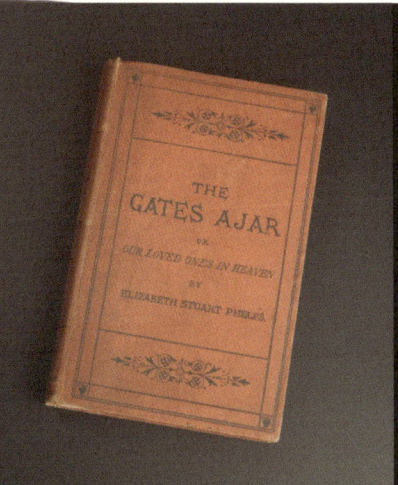

Elizabeth Stuart Phelps, *The Gates Ajar*, Ward, Lock & Tyler, 1870.
(The Collection of Louise and Barry Taper)

Mary Lincoln's personal copy inscribed "Mary Lincoln, September 1870." This popular spiritualist tract gave great comfort to Mary as evidenced in her recommending it to her close friend Eliza Slataper in a letter, November 7, 1870.

FIRST LADY OF CONTROVERSY 75

5

Feeling the need of a change of air, and indeed of every thing to restore me to health, you can well imagine, how restless I am feeling, awaiting the movements of a slow & I sometimes fear an indifferent agent. I should be now abroad,

Mary Lincoln, autograph letter signed,
to Benjamin Richardson, November 7, 1870.
(The Collection of Louise and Barry Taper)

Mary relates that Tad has learned German and forgotten his English. She also lovingly notes Tad "is growing very much like his dear father and possesses his great amiability of character and nobleness of nature."

Silver Chocolate Pot.
(The Mary Todd Lincoln Home, Lexington, Kentucky)
This Tiffany silver chocolate pot was probably purchased
after Mary's return from Europe in 1871.

Photograph of Mary Lincoln.
(Abraham Lincoln Presidential Library and Museum)

Little is known about this image, but some
have dated it around 1869.

TRAGEDY AND INSANITY

TRAGEDY AND INSANITY

The *Russia* arrived in New York harbor on May 11, 1871. After spending a number of days in New York to shop, Mary and Tad departed for Chicago. At the train station, Robert met them with his wife and young daughter, also named Mary. Mary Todd Lincoln and Tad stayed briefly at Robert's house on Wabash Avenue but soon moved into the Clifton House. Tad had been fighting a cough, presumably the result of a cold acquired during the voyage. Unable to shake it, his illness became progressively worse. By mid-June Tad was sleeping upright in bed, unable to lie flat without choking on his own saliva. The doctors termed his illness pleurisy, offering Mary hope that Tad would recover. At eighteen years of age, Tad struggled to survive. As his lungs filled with fluid, there was little that anyone could do. On July 15, 1871, Tad Lincoln died, leaving only Robert remaining of the four Lincoln sons.

Mary attended services in Chicago but did not accompany the body to Springfield. That task was left to Robert, as it had been before with his father's and Willie's remains. Tad was placed in the Lincoln Tomb along with Eddie, Willie, and his father. Three months later, Mary would survive the Great Chicago Fire. The death of her youngest son and the destruction of the city she called home led her on an odyssey. Over the next several years she traveled to health spas in Waukesha, Wisconsin, and St. Catharines in Canada, and to visit a spiritualist center in St. Charles, Illinois.

In July 1873, Mary wrote out a will, undoubtedly despondent about the memory of Tad's death. She befriended Dr. Willis Danforth, who treated her for her bouts of insomnia by providing packets of chloral hydrate, or as Mary called them, "white powders." She also became very close to the charismatic and controversial Presbyterian minister David Swing and his family. Mary had a premonition that she would die in September of 1874, but the month passed without incident. Newly discovered letters from the time suggest that she may have been addicted to the sleeping medication that, in large doses, can produce insomnia and hallucinations. After assisting with the wedding of David Swing's daughter in the fall of 1874, Mary looked to the warmer climate of Florida for the winter.

Trouble arose on March 12, 1875, when Dr. Ralph N. Isham, the physician for Robert and his family, received urgent telegrams from Mary Todd Lincoln pleading with him to save her son at all costs while she hurried to reach Chicago before Robert died. In fact, Robert and his entire family were in perfect health. Meeting his mother at the train station, he booked her into the Grand Pacific Hotel and checked himself in to the adjoining room. It was later alleged that she wandered about in the hallways in her nightdress, and when Robert and a hotel employee tried to escort her back to the room she screamed, "You are going to murder me." She carried the bulk of her securities and government bonds in a skirt pocket, a practice that seemed odd and dangerous. She regaled Robert about how someone tried to poison her in Florida, and she went on shopping sprees buying things that seemed to lack purpose. Robert hired Pinkerton detectives to follow his mother and record her actions. Increasingly, Robert and those around him believed that it was necessary to commit his mother to a sanitarium.

The question of Mary Lincoln's insanity will always be the subject of speculation. Many see the actions of her son as thuggish and insensitive, essentially using his power and prestige to remove his mother from further public embarrassment. Others have believed that Mary showed signs of mental illness early in life that only became more pronounced over time. Both positions rely on selective uses of evidence, with the full historical record being more complex and less conclusive.

Illinois law required a trial by jury before declaring someone insane. On May 19, 1875, Mary was escorted into the Cook County court in Chicago to determine if she was competent to conduct her own affairs. Represented by Leonard Swett, Mary listened as physicians Dr. Isham and Dr. Danforth testified to her insanity, along with Dr. R. J. Patterson, who was considered one of the leading experts on mental illness. It did not take the jury long to concur with the experts that Mary was insane. Rather than commit his mother to the state mental health facility, Robert sent her to Bellevue Place, a private sanitarium, in Batavia, Illinois. Insanity was viewed at the time much as any other illness, meaning it could be cured with enough rest, healthy foods, and exercise. Bellevue offered a peaceful setting where Mary was given the freedom to walk the grounds, take carriage rides, and not have any medications.

Robert seemed to think that Bellevue was perfect for his mother. Mary had different ideas. She felt a deep sense of betrayal and enlisted the assistance of Myra and James Bradwell to help with her release. Myra was one of the first women to be admitted to the Illinois bar, and her husband was a judge. Using well-placed stories in the press to plead Mary's case, both Dr. Patterson and Robert were increasingly being painted as the villians before the public. Recently uncovered correspondence shows how active Myra Bradwell was in advancing Mary's claims. An agreement was reached, allowing Mary to leave Bellevue and live with her sister, Elizabeth Edwards, in Springfield, Illinois. After only four months at Bellevue, Mary left for Springfield in September 1875. On June 15, 1876, a second court hearing rendered a different verdict, restoring Mary's legal right to control her affairs.

Once restored to freedom, Mary penned an angry letter to Robert demanding that he return all he allegedly had taken from her. Robert, unwilling to create any more public embarrassment, did so, but kept a file with a bundle of letters. In it were his mother's letters from happier times sending the items to him and his wife. Robert did not want to fight with his mother in a public forum. Rather, he wanted posterity to know that he was not a thief.

After all the commotion, Mary desired nothing more than peace and solitude. Believing that she could find these feelings again in Europe, Mary left New York on October 1, 1876, for France.

**Robert Todd Lincoln, autograph letter signed,
to Gideon Welles, July 1, 1875.**
(The Collection of Louise and Barry Taper)

At the same time Mary is privately complaining about Robert's treatment of her, Robert reassures Gideon Welles that "my mother is in appearance more in comfort and happiness than she has been since my fathers death. I have been exceedingly fortunate in being able to procure for her proper care and treatment in a place where all the surroundings are of the most pleasant character…In the absence of all excitement there are no very pronounced insane actions, but her mind is very weak and she is utterly unfit to take care of herself."

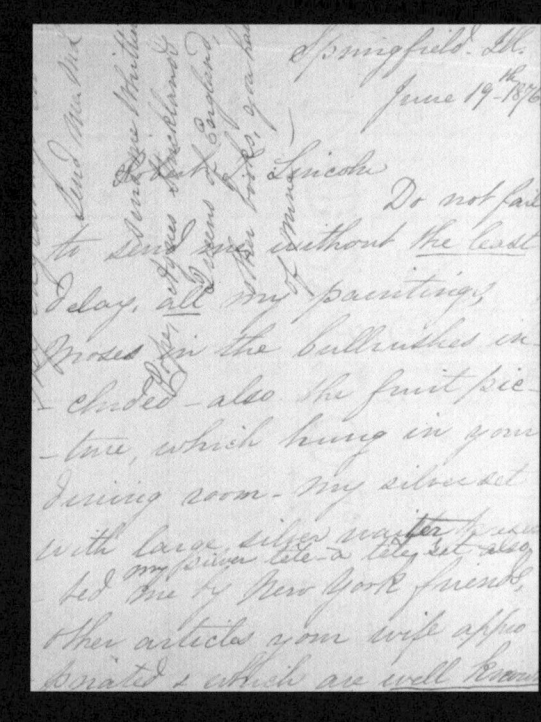

**Mary Lincoln, autograph letter signed,
to Robert T. Lincoln, June 19, 1876.**
(The Collection of Louise and Barry Taper)

Once legally restored to sanity, Mary wrote this angry letter demanding that Robert return all of the things she believed he stole from her including "all my paintings, Moses in the bullrushes included…also the fruit picture, which hung in your dining room…my silver set with large silver waiter presented me by New York friends, other articles your wife appropriated…"

Bed used by Mary Lincoln at Bellevue Place Sanitarium,
Batavia, Illinois.
(Batavia Historical Society)

Edward Bulwer-Lytton, *The Last Days of Pompeii*,
two volumes, Lippincott, 1860.
(The Collection of Louise and Barry Taper)

This 1834 novel, which she inscribed "Mary Lincoln 1864," is by Bulwer-Lytton, one of Mary's favorite authors. He is best known for penning the opening line "It was a dark and stormy night…" But Bulwer-Lytton, widely acclaimed as a historian and man of letters, was also devoted to spiritualism and incorporated its tenets into his novels. Mary possibly bought this right after an opera based on the novel appeared in 1863.

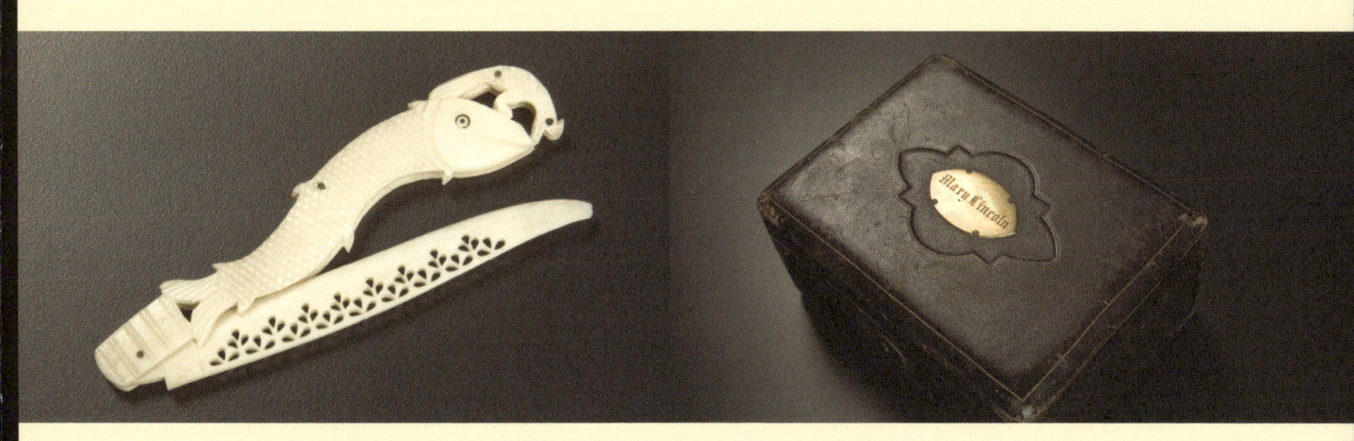

Ivory Letter Opener.
(The Collection of Louise and Barry Taper)

The ivory carved handle formed as a bird and fish reveals Mary's playful nature. Her known correspondence now totals over 700 letters.

Mary Lincoln Letter Box.
(The Collection of Louise and Barry Taper)

This black leather box contained many letters treasured by Mary Lincoln. An oval bronze plaque engraved "Mary Lincoln" is on the top, and a key lock on the front provided the security from prying eyes.

FIRST LADY OF CONTROVERSY

> Dec 24th
> Grand Central
>
> Dr Danforth
> My dear Sir:
> You certainly had not been gone 2 minutes, when Professor Swing was announced — and he mentioned that only five minutes before, had he received my note

> I hope you will sometimes meet him here — as he is the pleasantest company said "May I & ? Please write — call to see you? Please write — all these things, as much to them — him as I am sure you will — have

> you may believe that I greatly regretted the occurrence of your absence — for he made me, a most charming visit — How very few can appreciate such a noble man — If he was away from here, I should say, he had a grand career before him.

Mary Lincoln, autograph letter signed, to Dr. Willis Danforth, December 24 [1874?].
(Abraham Lincoln Presidential Library and Museum)

In this letter Mary mentions that Danforth missed meeting the Reverend David Swing by mere minutes, adding "I hope you will sometimes meet him here…"

Mary Lincoln, autograph letter signed, to Willis Danforth, circa fall 1874.
(Abraham Lincoln Presidential Library and Museum)

Mary writes to her physician "Please oblige me by sending about 4 more powders. I had a miserable night last night & took the 5 you left. What is to become of this excessive wakefulness, it is impossible for me to divine." The white powders refer to chloral hydrate, a crystalline substance used to induce sleep. Used in excess, it could cause addiction, insomnia, and hallucinations.

> Dr Danforth
> Please oblige me by sending about 4 more powders — I had a miserable night last night & took the 5 you left —

Mary Todd Lincoln

Abraham Lincoln, autograph note signed, to J. E. Allen, April 7, 1864.
(Abraham Lincoln Presidential Library and Museum)

Lincoln's request of Allen as Superintendent of Repair Shops was simple: "Shoe Tad's horse for him." It was common for Abraham and Mary Lincoln to use their influence to get an adult to do something for Tad.

The Poetical Works of Henry Wadsworth Longfellow, two volumes.

(Abraham Lincoln Presidential Library and Museum)

Mary inscribed these volumes "To Mary Ann Swing, December 25, 1873." Mary Ann Swing was the daughter of the Reverend David and Elizabeth Swing. David Swing was the charismatic minister at the Fourth Presbyterian Church of Chicago and a friend of Mary Lincoln.

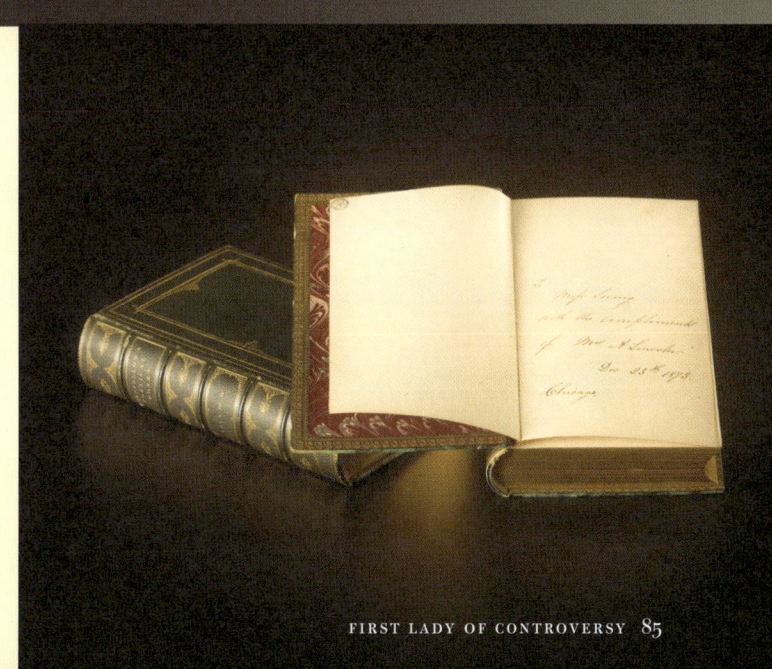

FIRST LADY OF CONTROVERSY 85

Lithographic print of Mary Lincoln circa 1862.
(Abraham Lincoln Presidential Library and Museum)

FROM PAU TO SPRINGFIELD

FROM PAU TO SPRINGFIELD

Mary found solace in the resort city of Pau, France, located at the base of the Pyrenees. Known for its health spas, Pau was so popular that a colony of English-speaking residents congregated there. Mary's fluency in French allowed her to converse with resident and visitor alike. She continued to travel throughout the continent but kept Pau as her base. Problems frequently arose in getting her pension check, which explains why most of the extant correspondence for this period is with Jacob Bunn, her Springfield banker and money manager. She also took a great fancy to her sister Elizabeth's 17-year-old grandson, Edward Lewis Baker, Jr. During her stay at Elizabeth's home, Mary and Edward became fast friends, in large part because he reminded Mary so much of Tad. Almost all of Mary's known letters from 1877 until her death in 1882 are to Bunn or Baker.

While Pau provided a place of retreat from the prying eyes of the world, it also afforded Mary some ease from the many health issues that had dogged her over the years. Urinary complaints increased as the result of damage done by her many pregnancies. She suffered from diabetes, cataracts, and edema. Several falls injured an already arthritic back. Spas could provide temporary relief, but it increasingly became evident that she would need the constant care only family provided at the time.

She departed from Europe on October 16, 1880, aboard the steamer *Amerique*. The famous actress Sarah Bernhardt recalled preventing a woman from falling down the steps of the ship after being unexpectedly rocked by a swell. The woman saved from a tumble down the steps was Mary Lincoln. Bernhardt recalled the exchange: "'You might have been killed, madame,' I said, 'down that horrible staircase!' 'Yes,' she answered, with a sigh of regret, 'but it was not God's will.'"

Mary spent the remainder of the year at her sister Elizabeth Edwards's house in Springfield, renting from Elizabeth the four rooms she used as her residence. Health problems forced her to seek relief at the spas at St. Catharines, Canada, and then in New York at Dr. Miller's Home of Health. In May 1881 newspapers reported a visit to his mother by Robert and his daughter, Mary. If reconciliation between mother and son occurred, this event would have provided the opportunity. Mary heard about efforts to increase her pension, largely due to the dire financial straits of Mrs. Garfield and her five children. Congress voted to increase the pensions of presidents' widows from $3,000 to $5,000. In addition, a one-time gift of $15,000 was provided.

By late March 1882, Mary had returned to Springfield from New York, taking up residence again in the Edwards home. Elizabeth recruited the assistance of the Third Order of Saint Francis, whose sisters helped Mary through her final days. On July 16, 1882, Mary Todd Lincoln died. Her funeral was held at the First Presbyterian Church. The casket was rosewood at her request. She had longed to join her husband and be at peace. Now she was reunited with him in death.

French Porcelain Inkwell.
(Abraham Lincoln Presidential Library and Museum)

Purchased during her European travels, this porcelain inkwell is one of several used by Mary Lincoln.

Ten Silver Bouillon Spoons.
(The Collection of Louise and Barry Taper)
Made by the Gorham Manufacturing Company, these silver bouillon soup spoons have Mary's monogram "ML" engraved on the handle.

[4 Oct 1882]

AN INVENTORY.

Of the Real and Personal Estate of *Mary Lincoln*, Deceased.

Personal Property

United States Registered 4% Bonds — par value — 72 000 00

Currency — 555 00

Personal effects — estimated value — 500

Real Estate
=None=

Robert T. Lincoln
Administrator

Inventory from Mary Lincoln Estate File, October 4, 1882.
(Abraham Lincoln Presidential Library and Museum)

Like Abraham Lincoln, Mary Lincoln died without a will. Robert was sole heir and became administrator of the estate. On the inventory, he lists all of Mary's personal property and real estate.

GRAND CENTRAL HOTEL,

New York, Feb 24th 1882,

My dear Mr Miner:

I wrote you several days since requesting you to write at once to Mr Springer regarding my new Pension paper & the $15000 — which both houses of Congress unanimously voted me — Where is the Money —

Mary Lincoln, autograph letter signed,
to Noyes W. Miner, February 24, 1882.
(Abraham Lincoln Presidential Library and Museum)

Mary writes to the Reverend Noyes W. Miner, the brother of her old friend Hannah Shearer, to solicit his help in obtaining the $15,000 one-time Congressional increase in her pension.

GRAND CENTRAL HOTEL

New York, March 21st 1882.

My dear Lewis:

May I request you to have a supervision over a box containing an invalid's chair & a smaller box also a very small package of medicine. I leave here tomorrow

GRAND CENTRAL HOTEL

New York, _____ 188_

2

Wednesday evening at 5½ o'clock — for Springfield — & find that I must rest from the Electric Baths, for a few weeks — I go west by way of Hudson River Railroad — to

Mary Lincoln, autograph letter signed,
to Edward Lewis Baker, Jr., March 21, 1882.
(Abraham Lincoln Presidential Library and Museum)

The last known letter written by Mary is to her nephew Edward Lewis Baker, Jr. In it, Mary requests that Baker have "supervision over a box containing an invalid's chair…" She also provides her itinerary for returning to Springfield where she would rent rooms from her sister

Lithograph print based upon Mathew B. Brady photograph, 1861.
(Abraham Lincoln Presidential Library and Museum)
This stylized print takes a studio photograph
and places Mary into an outdoor setting.

The nineteenth-century practice of sealing letters with melted wax embossed with a personalized seal was made easier by a long-handled tool such as this one. Mary's initials are on the metal seal. The embossed initials are reproduced on the cover of this catalog.